Fish and Shellfish Menus

Great Meals in Minutes was created by Rebus Inc., and
published by Time-Life Books.

This edition published 1995 by Bloomsbury Books, an
imprint of The Godfrey Cave Group, 42 Bloomsbury Street,
London, WC1B 3QJ.

© 1995 Time-Life Books BV.

ISBN 1 85471 561 5

Printed and bound in Great Britain.

Fish and Shellfish Menus

Leslie Land

Menu 1
Steamed Lobster with Four Sauces — 8
Sautéed New Cabbage
Oven-Fried Potatoes

Menu 2
Grilled Shark Steaks with Lime-Parsley Sauce — 10
Rice with Walnuts
Grilled Vegetables

Menu 3
Lemon-Braised Celery, Endive, and Watercress — 13
Haddock with Crab Meat and Hazelnut Stuffing

Paul Neuman and Stacy Bogdonoff

Menu 1
Poached Salmon with Green Sauce — 18
Rice Pilaf with Scallions
Asparagus with Lemon Glaze

Menu 2
Mediterranean Fish-Stew — 20
Basil Toasts
Watercress and Endive Salad with Warm Olive Oil
  Dressing

Menu 3
Grilled Swordfish with Herb Butter — 23
Sautéed Spinach with Shallots
New Potatoes Braised in Broth with Leeks

Patricia Unterman

Menu 1
Avocado and Grapefruit Salad with Walnut
  Oil Dressing — 28
Creole Fish and Oyster Stew
Baked Rice with Almonds

Menu 2
Fish Baked in Parchment with Red Peppers — 30
Polenta with Butter and Cheese
Marinated Salad

Menu 3
Fresh Tomato and Fennel Soup — 33
Trout Baked in Course Salt/Chard in Butter and Garlic
New Potatoes with Basil

Josephine Araldo

Menu 1
Quenelles with Shallot Sauce — 38
Potatoes with Onions and Cheese
Sautéed Carrots and Grapes

Menu 2
Avocado and Potato Soup — 40
Fillets of Sole in Wine Sauce
Courgette Merveille

Menu 3
Lime Bean Soup — 43
Whiting with Lemon Sauce
Cucumbers and Brussels Sprouts

Bruce Cliborne

Menu 1
Sautéed Scallops with White Wine Sauce — 48
Spicy Spinach Sauté
Wild Mushroom Salad with Basil and Mint

Menu 2
Mussels and Shrimp in Coconut Cream with Mint — 50
Stuffed Kohlrabi

Menu 3
Clams in Sesame-Ginger Sauce — 52
Fettuccine with Garlic and Oil
Mixed Vegetables, Oriental Style

Kathleen Kenny Sanderson

Menu 1
Seafood Soup Provençale — 56
Chèvre Florentine
Garlic Bread

Menu 2
Rainbow Trout — 57
Julienned Vegetables
Saffron Rice Mould

Menu 3
Sea Bass with Fennel Butter Sauce — 59
Warm Potato Salad
Garden Salad with Mustard Vinaigrette

Bloomsbury Books
London

Leslie Land

Menu 1
(*Left*)
Steamed Lobster with Four Sauces
Sautéed New Cabbage
Oven-Fried Potatoes

Living in an isolated coastal area in Maine, Leslie Land does not have the array of ingredients on hand that urban cooks do. But she finds this no hardship. Mail order brings non-perishable goods such as chilies and exotic canned foods, and a fisherman neighbour supplies her with freshly caught seafood. Her two gardens, where she raises four different kinds of strawberries, yield abundant seasonal vegetables, and she gathers her own wild mushrooms.

If seasons and a limited market place dictate how and what she cooks, Leslie Land nonetheless enjoys adding the unexpected and unconventional. Menu 1, a summer-autumn dinner, features a Maine favourite, steamed lobsters. With them she offers butter sauce, embellished with orange and lemon zests, allspice, and gin. In addition, she offers three other dipping mixtures, not only for the lobsters but also for the fried potatoes and sautéed cabbage. For Menu 3, she stuffs a whole boned and cleaned haddock with ground hazelnuts, crab meat, and currants.

The shark steak entrée of Menu 2 is itself an unusual offering. Shark meat is delicious; steaks from mako sharks, one of the most prevalent varieties sold for food, look and taste like swordfish. Sharks are common in many international dishes. To accompany the shark steaks, Leslie Land serves a nutty brown rice and grilled skewered fresh vegetables.

When you serve this informal company meal, place a boiled lobster and a portion of sautéed cabbage on each guest's plate. Serve the potatoes in a separate container, and set out individual ramekins with the four different dipping sauces within easy reach.

Steamed Lobster with Four Sauces
Sautéed New Cabbage
Oven-Fried Potatoes

Four dipping sauces accompany this meal; they are meant not only for the lobsters but also for the potatoes and cabbage. Two of these sauces are Japanese: one, *tempura*, contains garlic, ginger, and tamari, a rich mellow soy sauce often available in speciality food stores and health food shops. The other, *wasabi* sauce, is made from powdered grated wasabi, a strong, nose-tingling green horseradish-like condiment available in Oriental markets and speciality food shops. Regular Western horseradish is not a substitute.

What to drink
Boiled lobster needs a crisp, dry wine; try a California Sauvignon Blanc or Fumé Blanc.

Start-to-Finish Steps
1   Follow potatoes recipe steps 1 to 4.
2   Follow cabbage recipe steps 1 to 3.
3   Follow potatoes recipe steps 5 to 7.
4   Follow tempura sauce recipe steps 1 to 3 and sour cream sauce recipe steps 1 to 3.
5   Follow lobster recipe step 1 and citrus butter recipe step 1.
6   Follow lobster recipe step 2.
7   While lobsters are steaming, follow cabbage recipe step 4 and prepare wasabi sauce.
8   Follow citrus butter recipe step 2 and cabbage recipe step 5.
9   Follow lobster recipe step 3 and citrus butter recipe steps 3 and 4.
10   While completing citrus butter, follow potatoes recipe steps 8 and 9.
11   Follow lobster recipe step 4 and serve with cabbage and potatoes.

Steamed Lobster with Four Sauces

1½ teaspoons salt
4 live 'chicken' lobsters (each about 625 g (1¼ lbs))
Sour cream sauce (see following recipe)
Spiced citrus butter (see folowing recipe)
Tempura sauce (see following recipe)
Wasabi (see folowing recipe)

1   To stockpot large enough to hold all 4 lobsters without crowding, add enough water to come 13 to 15 cm (5 to 6 inches) up sides. Add salt, cover pan, and bring to a boil over high heat.
2   With water at full rolling boil, plunge in lobsters, one at a time, head first, and cover pan. Adjust heat so that water simmers but does not boil.. Cook 12 minutes from time last lobster goes in.
3   Remove pan from heat. With tongs, remove lobsters from water and drain. With chef's knife, slit shell on underbelly and crack lobster claws with nutcracker.
4   Place each lobster on a dinner plate and serve with the 4 sauces on the side.

Sour Cream Sauce

1 bunch fresh dill, or 1 level tablespoon dried
1 teaspoon cider vinegar or rice vinegar
1 tablespoon plus 1 teaspoon Dijon mustard
125 ml (4 fl oz) sour cream
½ teaspoon salt
3 to 4 tablespoons milk

1   If using fresh dill, rinse and pat dry with paper towels. With chef's knife, mince enough leaves and tender stems to measure 30 g (1 oz), and place in small bowl. If using dried, sprinkle with vinegar and crush with fork to blend.
2   With fork, stir in vinegar, if it has not already been added, mustard, sour cream, and salt, stirring until blended. Slowly stir in enough milk to give sauce texture of heavy cream.
3   Turn into small ramekin, cover, and set aside.

Spiced Citrus Butter

1 lemon
Large juice orange
6 level tablespoons salted butter
¹/₄ teaspoon ground allspice
1 tablespoon gin

1 Wash lemon and orange, and pat dry with paper towels. On fine holes of grater, shred enough peel to measure 1 level tablespoon lemon zest and 2 tablespoons orange zest. Halve lemon and orange. Squeeze enough lemon juice to measure 2 level tablespoons, and enough orange juice to measure 60 ml (2 fl oz). Strain to remove pits.
2 In small saucepan used for potatoes, melt butter over medium heat. Add allspice and citrus zests, and cook, stirring occasionally, 4 to 5 minutes.
3 With wooden spoon, stir in juices and blend thoroughly. Raise heat to medium-high and bring sauce to a boil.
4 Let sauce bubble rapidly 2 to 3 minutes. Stir in gin, pour into small ramekin, and serve.

Tempura Sauce

Large clove garlic
2¹/₂ cm (1 inch) piece fresh ginger (about 15 g (¹/₂ oz))
2 teaspoons brown sugar
3 tablespoons dry sherry
2 tablespoons tamari or other aged soy sauce, preferably, or 1 tablespoon plus 1 teaspoon regular soy sauce

1 Peel garlic and ginger. On fine holes of grater, shred garlic, letting shreds fall into ramekin. You should have about 1 tablespoon. Shred ginger in same manner.
2 Add sugar, sherry, and tamari, stirring well after each addition until sugar is dissolved.
3 Cover, and set aside until ready to serve.

Wasabi Sauce

2 tablespoons wasabi

1 Place 2 tablespoons wasabi on saucer.
2 Slowly stir in water, a drop or two at a time, until sauce is texture of heavy cream. It will thicken as it stands.
3 Turn into small ramekin, cover loosely, and set aside.

Sautéed New Cabbage

Medium-size head green cabbage, preferably new crop (about 750 g (1¹/₂ lbs))
2 level tablespoons salted butter
¹/₂ teaspoons salt

1 Remove coarse, limp outer leaves from cabbage.
2 Quarter cabbage and remove core. If core is tender and sweet, cut into 5 mm (¹/₄ inch) dice; if tough, discard.
3 Using chef's knife or grater, shred cabbage as for slaw. Place shreds in large bowl and set aside.
4 In large heavy-gauge skillet, melt butter over medium heat. As soon as butter turns brown, add cabbage, a handful at a time. Raise heat to medium-high and cook, stirring frequently with wooden spoon, until cabbage is tender but still crisp, 8 to 10 minutes.
5 Stir in salt, reduce heat to very low, and keep warm.

Oven-Fried Potatoes

4 large baking potatoes (about 1¹/₄ kg (2¹/₂ lbs) total weight)
1 level tablespoon salted butter
100 ml (3 fl oz) vegetable oil
Salt

1 Preheat oven to 230°C (450°F or Mark 8).
2 In small saucepan, bring 750 ml (1¹/₂ pts) water to a boil over high heat.
3 Peel potatoes and cut lengthwise into 8 mm (¹/₃ inch) thick slabs. Cut slabs crosswise into 1¹/₂ cm (³/₄ inch) thick French fries. In shallow roasting pan, arrange potatoes in single layer.
4 Pull oven rack out slightly and place pan on it. Pour in enough boiling water to cover, about 500 ml (1 pt). Carefully slide rack and pan into oven and bake 10 minutes.
5 Remove pan from oven and carefully pour off water.
6 Add butter and oil to potatoes and, with metal spatula, stir and toss until butter has melted and potatoes are coated evenly.
7 Return potatoes to oven and bake until crisp and well browned, about 35 to 40 minutes, stirring often with spatula and loosening any that stick to bottom of pan.
8 Transfer potatoes to paper-towel-lined platter and sprinkle generously with salt.
9 Turn potatoes into napkin-lined basket and serve.

Choose large plates to accomodate the grilled fish steak, garnished with lime 'wheels', the skewered grilled vegetables, and a serving of brown rice and walnuts. Serve any extra lime-parsley sauce in a small pitcher.

Shark meat – still a bargain – is a firm, dry, delicately flavoured fish that many U.S. consumers overlook. The most popular varieties are the dark-fleshed mako and blue sharks. If you cannot find shark, use any other firm fleshed fish like halibut or swordfish. Shark meat often has a mildly ammoniac taste; it requires brief soaking in a vinegar or citrus juice mixture to neutralize it.

Brown rice is unpolished white rice with its bran coating intact. The nutty flavour of the brown rice is complemented here by sautéed walnuts.

Let seasonal availability dictate your ingredient selection for the grilled vegetables. Instead of squash, the cook suggests substituting either red or green bell peppers, or long slender Japanese eggplant.

What to drink
Serve a soft wine with medium body and a touch of sweetness: a dry Chenin Blanc or French Colombard from California, or a dry Vouvray from France.

Start-to-Finish Steps
At least 30 minutes ahead: Soak bamboo skewers in water to prevent scorching.

1 Follow rice recipe step 1.
2 While rice is cooking, follow grilled vegetable recipe step 1. For shark recipe, mince parsley, slice ginger, squeeze lime juice, and, if using, cut lime 'wheels' for garnish.
3 For rice recipe, grate lime zest, mince garlic, and mince scallion tops or snip chives for garnish, if using. Follow rice recipe step 2.
4 Follow shark recipe steps 1 and 2.
5 Follow rice recipe step 3.
6 Follow vegetables recipe step 2.
7 Follow rice recipe step 4 and vegtables recipe step 3.
8 Follow shark recipe step 3.
9 Follow vegetables recipe step 4 and rice recipe step 5.
10 Follow shark recipe steps 4 through 8 and vegetables recipe step 5.
11 Follow shark recipe step 9 and rice recipe step 6.
12 Follow shark recipe step 10, rice recipe step 7, and serve with vegetables.

Grilled Shark Steaks with Lime-Parsley Sauce

2 tablespoons tamari, preferably, or other aged soy sauce
$1/2$ teaspoon ground cumin
60 g (2 oz) minced fresh parsley
125 ml (4 fl oz) lime juice
250 ml (8 fl oz) olive oil
5 cm (2 inch) piece of fresh ginger, cut into $2^{1}/_{2}$ mm ($^{1}/_{8}$ inch) thick slices.
4 shark, bluefin tuna, albacore, swordfish, or catfish steaks (each 250 g (8 oz))
350 ml (12 fl oz) sour cream
1 lime, thinly sliced into 'wheels' for garnish (optional)

1 Preheat grill and set grill rack as close as possible to heating element.
2 For basting sauce, combine tamari, cumin, parsley, lime juice, olive oil, and ginger in small bowl. With fork, stir to combine. Set aside.
3 Wipe steaks with damp paper towels. Brush one side of each steak with oil that has risen to top of reserved basting sauce, and arrange fish, oiled-sides down, in centre of disposable grill pan. Brush top sides with oil.
4 Grill fish 8 to 10 minutes. Do not turn. Fish is done when it flakes easily when tested with a fork and is opaque all through.
5 Remove ginger from marinade and purée remainder of sauce in food processor or blender.
6 In small saucepan, bring sauce to a simmer over medium heat, stirring occasionally, 2 to 3 minutes.
7 Place sour cream in medium-size bowl and gradually add warmed sauce, stirring until blended.
8 Remove fish from grill, cover loosely with aluminium foil, and keep warm on stove top.
9 Add pan juices to the sauce and stir to combine.
10 Divide steaks among 4 dinner plates and top each with a garnish of lime 'wheels' if desired. Serve remaining sauce separately.

Rice with Walnuts

175 g (6 oz) brown rice
½ teaspoon salt
3 level tablespoons salted butter
Large clove garlic, minced
3 level tablespoons grated lime zest (about 2 large
  limes)
125 g (4 oz) coarsely broken walnuts
60 g (2 oz) minced scallion tops or 3 level
  tablespoons snipped chives for garnish (optional)

1 In small heavy-gauge saucepan, bring 500 ml (1 pt) water to a boil over high heat. Stir in rice and salt. Return to a boil, cover pan, reduce heat to low, and cook rice 40 minutes, or until all water is absorbed and rice is tender.
2 In small skillet, melt butter over medium heat. Add garlic and lime zest and sauté, stirring often, until garlic is golden and zest smells toasty, about 5 minutes.
3 Stir in walnuts and continue to sauté, stirring frequently with wooden spoon, until walnuts are golden brown, 5 to 8 minutes more.
4 Remove pan from heat and cover to keep warm until rice is done.
5 Remove rice from heat. Covered rice will keep at least 15 minutes.
6 Add walnut mixture to rice and, with fork, toss gently until combined.
7 Divide rice among 4 plates and garnish with chives or scallion tops, if desired.

Grilled Vegetables

Large yellow summer squash (about 500 g (1 lb))
Large courgette (about 125 g (¼ lb))
Large bunch scallions
8 large mushrooms (125 to 150 g (4 to 5 oz))
1 tablespoon olive oil, approximately

1 Rinse both squashes and pat dry with paper towels. With chef's knife, halve lengthwise and cut into 2½ cm (1 inch) rounds. Trim scallions, leaving about 2½ cm (1 inch) of the green, and cut into 5 cm (2 inch) lengths. Reserve green tops for rice recipe, if using for garnish. Wipe mushrooms with damp paper towels and halve.
2 Thread vegetables onto bamboo skewers, alternating scallions, mushrooms, courgette, and summer squash. Skewer mushrooms through the cap, rather than through the stem, to prevent them from splitting.
3 Brush vegetables lightly with oil, place in disposable grill pan, and grill about 2 minutes per side.
4 Remove vegetables from grill, cover loosely with foil, and keep warm on stove top.
5 Uncover vegetables, return to grill, and grill additional 2 minutes per side, or just until tender and lightly speckled with brown.

Leftover suggestion
Leftover rice and shark steak can be combined for a simple luncheon salad the following day. Flake the fish, then moisten it with any leftover sauce or with freshly squeezed lime juice. Add the fish to the cold rice and toss. To further enhance the salad, add cubes of ham, cooked and cooled shellfish, or any cut-up fresh or leftover cooked vegetables. Garnish the salad with walnuts or with croutons, if desired.

Lemon-Braised Celery, Endive, and Watercress
Haddock with Crab Meat and Hazelnut Stuffing

Garnish the stuffed haddock with lemon 'wheels' and parsley sprigs. Serve the vegetables separately.

For the haddock entrée, ask the fish dealer to clean, bone, and butterfly the fish for you, leaving on its head and tail. Check the fish carefully for small bones as you eat it. If haddock is not available, use rock cod, sea bass, or any other mild, white-fleshed fish.

Look for hazelnuts, also known as filberts, in speciality food shops or health food stores. Toasting the hazelnuts is a simple process that brings out their delicate flavour fully. After the nuts cool, rub off their bitter skins, several nuts at a time, with a kitchen towel.

Currants, smaller, harder, and stronger-tasting than raisins, are a variety of tiny black grapes that are dried.

You may substitiute chopped dark raisins, but their flavour and texture are different.

Whether you use fresh or frozen crab meat, carefully pick out any bits of shell or cartilage before adding the crab to the filling mixture.

Celery hearts, the cluster of inner ribs, should be crisp and have fresh-looking leaves. Endive and watercress, both slightly bitter greens, are good flavour foils for the bland celery. Slender, tapered heads of Belgian endive should be firm and crisp, with ivory leaves fringed in pale yellow.

Watercress should look fresh and bright green.

Braising, an ideal way to cook the endive and the celery, both mellows and tenderizes them. The watercress, added during the last five minutes of cooking, retains its crisp texture and bright colour.

The haddock is presented whole on a bed of extra filling. Carefully lift the fish from its baking pan with two spatulas so that it does fall apart. Serve the fish and the vegetables on separate plates to prevent the mixing of the fish juices with the vegetable juices.

What to drink

Because of the richness of the haddock stuffing, a full-bodied wine is advisable. Choose a California Chardonnay or a white Burgundy, such as a Mâcon or St. Veran.

Start-to-Finish Steps

1 Follow haddock recipe steps 1 and 2.
2 While hazelnuts are toasting, halve baguette (reserving other half for celery recipe), cut into 3 or 4 pieces, and, in food processor or blender, reduce to large crumbs. Follow haddock recipe step 3.
3 Wash parsley and pat dry with paper towels. Strip enough leaves from stems to measure 30 g (1 oz), reserving several sprigs for garnish, if desired. Chop raisins, if using. Follow haddock recipe steps 4 through 13.
4 Squeeze enough lemon to measure 1 tablespoon

juice and follow celery recipe steps 1 through 3.
5 While endive and celery are cooking, slice remaining half of French bread and set aside. For haddock recipe, slice lemon 'wheels' for garnish, if using.
6 Follow celery recipe step 4 and haddock recipe step 14, turning oven to grill as soon as you remove fish.
7 Follow celery recipe steps 5 and 6, haddock recipe steps 15 and 16, and serve.

Lemon-Braised Celery, Endive, and Watercress

2 bunches celery
4 medium-size Belgian endives (500 to 625 g (1 to 1¼ lbs) total weight)
Large bunch watercress
Large clove garlic
2 level tablespoons salted butter
1 tablespoon lemon juice
Twelve 1 cm (½ inch) slices French baguette or long Italian bread

1 Remove outer stalks of celery and keep for another use. Separate celery heart stalks, and trim bases. Rinse under cold water and pat dry with paper towels. Remove wilted outer leaves from endive. Pick over watercress, discarding any yellowed or wilted leaves as well as tough lower stems. In colander, rinse endive and watercress under cold running water and dry in salad spinner or pat dry with paper towels.
2 With chef's knife, cut celery pieces 3½ cm (1½ inches) long and 1 cm (½ inch) wide. Leave the leaves on the innermost stalks. Cut endive lengthwise into quarters. Peel garlic.
3 In skillet used for stuffing, melt butter over medium heat. With garlic press, crush garlic into skillet and cook, stirring with wooden spoon, 1 to 2 minutes. Add celery and endive, turning gently to coat with butter. Add lemon juice, reduce heat to medium-low, cover pan, and cook 5 to 6 minutes.
4 Uncover pan and gently stir in watercress. Raise heat to medium and, stirring frequently, continue to cook uncovered about 5 minutes, or until vegetables are crisp tender.
5 Arrange bread slices on grill rack and place in preheated grill. Toast bread until golden, 1½ to 2 minutes per side. Transfer to napkin-lined basket.
6 Turn vegetables into serving dish and serve with toast on individual side dishes.

Haddock with Crab Meat and Hazelnut Stuffing

100 g (3 oz) hazelnuts
3 level tablespoons salted butter, approximately
125 g (4 oz) coarse fresh bread crumbs
1 whole haddock 2¼ to 2½ kg (4¼ to 5 lbs),
    cleaned, boned, and butterflied, with head and
    tail left on
175 g (6 oz) cooked crabmeat
4 shallots
30 g (1 oz) parsley
½ teaspoon salt
1 tablespoon currants or chopped dark raisins
1 egg
250 ml (8 fl oz) dry white wine
Parsley sprigs for garnish (optional)
2 lemons, sliced into 'wheels' for garnish
    (optional)

1   Preheat oven to 180°C (350°F or Mark 4).
2   In pie plate, arrange nuts in single layer. Toast 12 minutes, or until skins have split open and meat is light, golden brown. Remove from oven and allow to cool. Raise oven temperature to 190°C (375°F or Mark 5).
3   In large non-aluminium skillet, melt 2 level tablespoons butter over medium heat. Add bread crumbs and fry, stirring occasionally with wooden spatula, until crumbs are golden brown. Remove pan from heat and set aside.
4   Rinse haddock inside and out under cold running water. With paper towels, wipe out bloodline from gut and pat fish dry.
5   In small bowl, pick over crabmeat, removing any shell or cartilage, and flake with fork. Set aside.
6   With paring knife, peel shallots. Using food processor or chef's knife, mince shallots and parsley. Transfer to medium-size bowl.
7   With kitchen towel, rub cooled hazelnuts to remove skins. A few brown spots will be left.
8   Turn hazelnuts into food processor and process until nuts are same size as large bread crumbs. Or, using blender, process in small batches. With rubber spatula, scrape hazelnuts into bowl containing shallot-parsley mixture. Add fried bread crumbs, salt, currants, crab meat, and egg, and stir to combine thoroughly. Wipe out skillet.
9   Lightly butter large roasting pan.
10 In small saucepan, melt 1 level tablespoon of butter over low heat.
11 Spread open body cavity of haddock and stuff it with as much of the crabmeat-hazelnut mixture as will fit comfortably and still allow the flaps of the cavity to close round it completely. Wrap leftover stuffing in aluminium foil and place in small baking dish.
12 With your hands or using 2 metal spatulas, place fish in buttered roasting pan, drizzle with melted butter, and pour wine around, but not over it.
13 Bake fish and foil-wrapped stuffing in upper third of preheated oven, 15 to 20 minutes, or until fish flakes easily when tested near thick part of the backbone with tip of knife.
14 Remove fish and stuffing packet from oven. Raise temperature of grill for bread.
15 Open packet and form a bed of stuffing on serving platter large enough to hold fish. Using 2 spatulas, carefully lift fish out and place on stuffing.
16 Cover eyes with parsley sprigs and garnish platter with lemon 'wheels' and parsley sprigs, if desired.

Paul Neuman and Stacy Bogdonoff

Menu 1
(Right)
Poached Salmon with Green Sauce
Rice Pilaf with Scallions
Asparagus with Lemon Glaze

Though Paul Neuman never trained as a cook, he has had extensive experience in the food business, including work at his family's Manhattan fish market. He and Stacy Bogdonoff, his wife, now run a Manhattan catering service. He believes that food preparation must be simple and direct. Most importantly, meals must be aesthetically appealing, with vidid, often contrasting, colours and textures – a concept he derived from Japanese cuisine.

With classical training in French cooking, Stacy Bogdonoff brings to his team the technical competence to produce *haute cuisine*. Nevertheless, she describes herself as an untraditional cook who, like her husband, prefers vivid, visual foods.

As they cook and plan menus together, they select a central element or ingredient, something they like to cook, and build the meal around that. They always follow a cardinal rule: plan a meal for flavour and visual impact. The themes for Menu 1 and Menu 3 are similar. Pale-fleshed fish steaks – salmon and swordfish – play off the bright greens of the vegetables and the pale greens of the fish sauces.

The dramatic fish chowder of Menu 2 is richly textured and colourful. Served in a shallow bowl, the mussel shells and chunks of seafood are half-covered with the orange-red liquid. The endive and watercress salad and the basil toast create additional textures and colours.

When you serve this elegant spring or summer meal, arrange the salmon steaks on a platter with the warm green sauce, and garnish with watercress sprigs. Pass the asparagus spears and the rice pilaf in separate dishes. If you have them, use white serving pieces to emphasize the various shades of green and white in this meal.

Poached Salmon with Green Sauce
Rice Pilaf with Scallions
Asparagus with Lemon Glaze

In this menu the main-course fish is cooked by poaching, a low-calorie cooking method that uses no fat. The barely simmering poaching liquid can contain many seasonings or may be flavoured only with lemon juice, as in this recipe. It must never boil because the rapid water movement would break the fish apart, marring both flavour and appearance. Firm-fleshed fish such as salmon (or its substitutes in this recipe, sea bass or striped bass) are best for poaching. Save 125 ml (4 fl oz) of poaching liquid for the accompanying sauce, and store the rest in the refrigerator or freezer for future use. The green sauce calls for fresh dill, but you can substitute parsley or basil.

Select plump, bright-green asparagus with compact tips. Before storing the spears, cut a small piece from the bottom of each, then stand them upright in a container of cold water in the refrigerator. If fresh asparagus are not available, use any green vegetable in season – perhaps broccoli, green beans, or snow peas.

What to drink
To complement the delicate salmon and sauce, choose a subtle wine such as a Reisling.

Start-to-Finish Steps
1   Follow pilaf recipe steps 1 and 2.
2   While vegetables are cooking, follow green sauce recipe steps 1 and 2 and salmon recipe step 1.
3   Follow green sauce recipe step 3.
4   While cream is reducing, follow pilaf recipe steps 3 and 4.
5   While stock is coming to a boil, follow salmon recipe steps 2 and 3.
6   Juice lemons for salmon and asparagus recipes. Follow salmon recipe step 4 and pilaf recipe step 5.
7   While pilaf is cooking, follow asparagus recipe steps 1 and 2.
8   Follow salmon recipe step 5 and green sauce recipe step 4.
9   While sauce is reducing, place serving platters for salmon and asparagus and bowl for pilaf in oven to warm and follow asparagus recipe step 3.
10 Follow green sauce recipe step 5 and asparagus recipe step 4.

11 Follow green sauce recipe step 6.
12 Follow asparagus recipe step 5, green sauce recipe step 7, pilaf recipe step 6, salmon recipe step 6, and serve.

Poached Salmon with Green Sauce

4 centre-cut fillets of salmon, sea bass, or striped bass, or 2½ cm (1 inch) thick steaks (each 250 g (8 oz))
125 ml (4 fl oz) lemon juice
Green sauce (see following recipe)
8 sprigs of watercress (optional)

1   Wipe salmon with damp paper towels.
2   In each of 2 large skillets, bring 5 cm (2 inches) water and 60 ml (2 fl oz) lemon juice to a boil over high heat. Reduce to a simmer.
3   Preheat oven to SLOW.
4   Add salmon in single layer, making sure fish is completely covered by liquid (add more water if necessary). Return water to a simmer and poach salmon, being careful not to boil, until fish turns light pink all the way through, 8 to 10 minutes. Using sharp stainless steel knife, make a small slit in centre of salmon to check colour.
5   With 1 or 2 slotted spatulas, transfer fish to heatproof plate and keep warm in preheated oven. Measure 125 ml (4 fl oz) poaching liquid and reserve for sauce. Discard remaining liquid. Rinse out 1 skillet.
6   Pour small amount of sauce on heated serving platter, top with salmon, and cover with remaining sauce. Garnish with sprigs of watercress, if desired.

Green Sauce

2 shallots
½ medium-size bunch watercress
Small bunch dill
250 ml (8 fl oz) heavy cream
3 tablespoons dry white wine
3 tablespoons sweet vermouth
125 ml (4 fl oz) reserved salmon poaching liquid
Salt and freshly ground black pepper
2 level tablespoons unsalted butter

1 Wash, peel, and finely mince shallots. Set aside.
2 In colander, wash watercress and dill. Dry in salad spinner or pat dry with paper towels. Remove stems and discard. In food processor or blender, combine watercress and dill, and process until smooth. Set aside.
3 In small saucepan, reduce cream by half over medium-high heat, about 10 to 15 minutes.
4 In small enamel-lined saucepan, combine wine, vermouth, poaching liquid, and shallots. Bring to a boil over medium-high heat, and cook until liquid is reduced by half, about 8 to 10 minutes.
5 Reduce heat to medium. Add reduced cream to wine mixture, whisking until blended, and cook just until sauce thickens, about 3 to 5 minutes.
6 With rubber spatula, scrape processed watercress and dill into sauce. Add salt and pepper to taste, and whisk until blended.
7 Remove pan from heat and add 1 tablespoon butter at a time, whisking until totally incorporated.

Rice Pilaf with Scallions

2 stalks celery
Medium-size bunch scallions
Large yellow onion
3 tablespoons vegetable oil
150 g (5 oz) long-grain white rice
350 ml (12 fl oz) chicken stock or water
Salt and freshly ground white pepper
30 g (1 oz) chopped parsley

1 Wash celery and scallions, and pat dry with paper towels. With chef's knife, trim off ends of celery and scallions and finely dice. Peel and dice onion.
2 In large skillet, heat oil over medium heat. Add celery and onion, and sauté, stirring frequently with wooden spatula, until vegetables are translucent, about 10 minutes.

3 Add scallions and rice, and sauté, stirring another 3 to 5 minutes.
4 Add stock or water, stir, and bring to a boil over high heat.
5 Cover, reduce heat to medium, and cook until rice is tender and has absorbed liquid, about 18 minutes. Remove pan from heat and keep covered until ready to serve.
6 Fluff rice with fork and season with salt and white pepper to taste. Turn into warmed serving bowl and sprinkle with parsley.

Asparagus with Lemon Glaze

16 spears fresh asparagus (about 500 g (1 lb) total weight), or 500 g (1 lb) green beans, broccoli, or snow peas
Medium-size bunch chives
125 g (4 oz) unsalted butter
100 ml (3 fl oz) lemon juice
1 tablespoon Dijon mustard
Salt and freshly ground black pepper

1 Wash asparagus and break off ends. Peel stems and, if necessary, trim ends to make spears of uniform length. Set aside. Wash, pat dry, and mince 30 g (1 oz) plus 1 teaspoon chives.
2 In small enamel-lined saucepan melt butter over low heat. Add lemon juice, 30 g (1 oz) chives, mustard, and salt and pepper to taste. Cover partially and keep warm over very low heat.
3 In large skillet used for salmon, bring 5 cm (2 inches) water to a boil over high heat.
4 Place asparagus in skillet, return water to a boil, and cook spears 4 to 5 minutes, until bright green and tender but still firm.
5 Drain asparagus in colander and place on warmed serving platter. Pour lemon butter over asparagus and garnish with remaining chives.

Mediterranean Fish Stew
Basil Toasts
Watercress and Endive Salad with Warm Olive Oil Dressing

The richly seasoned Mediterranean chowder contains vegetables, herbs, and four varieties of seafood. The mackerel for the chowder should be as fresh as possible. If none is available fresh, use frozen, but not canned. When buying live mussels, check that their shells are tightly closed. For any with open shells, test if they are alive by trying to slide the two shells laterally across one another. Discard any with shells

Garnish the appetizingly colourful Mediterranean fish stew with chopped parsley. To accompany this substantial entrée, pass crisp basil toasts and a salad of watercress and endive. Informal serving pieces are ideal.

that move or that remain open; also discard any mussels that do not open during cooking. Raw shrimp should be firm and odour free.

Since squid is usually sold whole, ask the fish dealer to clean it and cut it up.

Fresh fennel and saffron threads flavour the chowder base. Fennel has a delicate anise flavour; it is available in Italian groceries and some supermarkets. If fresh fennel is unavailable, use fennel seeds and four stalks of sliced celery. Grind saffron threads with a mortar and pestle or pulverize them with your fingers between two sheets of wax paper.

Basil toasts can be prepared up to five days in advance and stored in an air-tight container.

What to drink

Mediterranean flavours go with Mediterranean wines. Serve a French rosé, such as a Lirac or a Tavel, or a full-bodied Italian white, such as a Greco di Tufo.

Start-to-Finish Steps

1 Follow fish stew recipe steps 1 to 3.
2 While onions are sautéing, wash, dry, and chop basil for fish stew and basil toasts recipes. Grate Parmesan for basil toasts recipe.
3 Follow fish stew recipe step 4.
4 While tomato mixture is cooking, follow fish stew recipe step 5, basil toasts recipe steps 1 to 4, and salad recipe steps 1 to 3.
5 Follow basil toasts recipe step 5 and fish stew recipe step 6.
6 While fish is cooking, follow salad recipe steps 4 and 5.
7 Warm serving bowl and platter under hot running water. Dry. Follow fish stew recipe step 7, salad recipe step 6, and serve with basil toasts.

Mediterranean Fish Stew

2 large yellow onions
6 cloves garlic
1 fennel bulb, or 1 level tablespoon fennel seeds
1 teaspoon saffron threads
6 tablespoons olive oil
125 ml (4 fl oz) white burgundy wine
1 kg (2 lb) can Italian plum tomatoes
60 g (2 oz) tomato paste
1 level tablespoon chopped fresh basil, or 1 teaspoon dried
12 mussels
250 g (½ lb) medium-size fresh shrimp
500 g (1 lb) whole mackerel, boned
1 orange
2 squid (about 500 g (1 lb) total weight, cleaned and cut into rings
2 tablespoons choped fresh parsley for garnish (optional)

1 With chef's knife, peel and slice onions, and peel and chop garlic. Wash and slice fennel bulb, if using.

2 Using mortar and pestle or with fingers, crush saffron.

3 In large heavy-gauge saucepan or stockpot, heat oil over medium-high heat until hot but not smoking. Add onions and fresh fennel, if using. Sauté, stirring with wooden spoon, until onions are soft but not transparent, about 5 minutes. Add garlic, saffron, and wine. Cook 1 minute.

4 Add tomatoes, tomato paste, basil, and fennel seed, if using. Break up tomatoes with spoon. Cover, reduce heat to low, and cook 30 to 35 minutes.

5 With stiff brush, scrub mussels under cold running water. Pull of any beards. Shell and devein shrimp. Cut mackerel into 3½ cm (1½ inch) pieces. Finely grate enough orange rind to measure 2 tablespoons.

6 Stir in orange rind. Add mussels to tomato mixture and cook 2 minutes. Add shrimp and squid, then gently top with fish pieces. Cook 3 minutes. Turn off heat.

7 When ready to serve, gently ladle stew into serving bowl, so that fish pieces do not fall apart. If desired, garnish with chopped parsley.

Basil Toasts

2 or 3 shallots
1 long loaf crusty French bread
125 g (4 oz) unsalted butter
2 level tablespoons finely chopped fresh basil, or 2 teaspoons dried
30 g (1 oz) freshly grated Parmesan cheese

1 Preheat oven to 230°C (450°F or Mark 8).
2 With chef's knife, peel shallots and mince finely.
3 With serrated knife, cut bread into 1½ cm (¾ inch) thick slices and arrange in single layer on cookie sheet.
4 In small skillet, melt butter over low heat. Add shallots and sauté, stirring with wooden spatula, until just translucent, about 3 minutes. Add basil and stir to blend.
5 Brush bread slices with herb butter and sprinkle with cheese. Bake until lightly browned, 8 to 10 minutes.

Watercress and Endive Salad with Warm Olive Oil Dressing

2 bunches watercress
2 heads endive
1 lemon
125 ml (4 fl oz) olive oil
60 ml (2 fl oz) walnut oil
60 ml (2 fl oz) sherry vinegar or balsamic vinegar
1 egg
Salt
Freshly ground pepper

1 Wash watercress and remove stems. Dry in salad spinner or pat dry with paper towels
2 Remove bruised outer leaves of endive. With chef's knife, cut endive into 5 mm (¼ inch) thick diagonal slices, from tip to root end.
3 In salad bowl, combine watercress and endive. Cover and place in refrigerator. Squeeze enough lemon juice to measure 2 teaspoons.
4 In small saucepan, heat olive oil and walnut oil over medium heat just until warm. Off heat, add vinegar and lemon juice. Remove pits, if necessary.
5 In small bowl, separate egg, retaining yolk and discarding white. In a slow, steady stream, add oil and vinegar mixture, whisking constantly until sauce is smooth and thick. Season with salt and pepper to taste.
6 Remove greens from refrigerator, toss with dressing, and serve.

Grilled Swordfish with Herb Butter
Sautéed Spinach with Shallots
New Potatoes Braised in Broth with Leeks

Sautéed spinach with a twist of orange rind, together with new potatoes braised with leeks, provide appealing colour contrasts to the swordfish steaks, which are capped with medallions of herb butter.

Swordfish has firm flesh and a flavour that can stand alone without elaborate sauces or seasonings. An uncomplicated herb butter, is in fact, the ideal sauce. Make the butter in advance, if you prefer, and store it, for up to 3 days in the refrigerator or up to 6 weeks in the freezer, rolled in a log shape and wrapped in wax paper. To serve, slice rounds from the roll and place on top of the fish steaks just before serving.

The sautéed spinach dish calls for shallots, considered the aristocrat of onions because of their very delicate flavour. The spinach is tossed with a medley of citrus juices – lemon, orange, and lime – which add a subtle flavour to the dish.

Buy straight, slender leeks, avoiding those that have become bulbous, as they may be woody and flavourless. Choose those with the greenest tops and wash them thoroughly. Coarse mustard, an essential flavouring ingredient in the stock, contains crushed mustard seeds, unlike Dijon mustards. Imported and domestic mustards are sold in most supermarkets.

What to drink

These dishes are simple and direct, and the wine should match them; choose a Californian Pinot Blanc, a dry Vouvray from the Loire, or a white Burgundy.

Start-to-Finish Steps

At least 1 hour ahead: Follow herb butter recipe steps 1 through 3.

1 Follow spinach recipe steps 1 and 2.
2 Follow potatoes recipe steps 1 to 5.
3 Follow swordfish recipe steps 1 and 2.
4 Follow potatoes recipe step 6 and swordfish recipe step 3. Warm plates under hot running water.
5 Follow swordfish recipe step 4, potatoes recipe step 7, and spinach recipe steps 3 to 5.
6 Follow swordfish recipe step 5. While steaks finish grilling, dry plates.
7 Follow swordfish recipe step 6, potato recipe step 8, and spinach recipe step 6 and serve.

Grilled Swordfish with Herb Butter

Four 2½ cm (1 inch) thick swordfish steaks (each about 250 g (8 oz)
60 ml (2 fl oz) olive oil
Herb butter (see following recipe)

1 Preheat grill. Place grill pan 7½ to 10 cm (3 to 4 inches) from heating element and heat 3 to 5 minutes.
2 Wipe swordfish with damp paper towels. Lightly brush both sides of steaks with oil.
3 Place steaks on grill pan and grill 4 to 5 minutes.
4 Using metal spatula, turn steaks and grill 2 to 3 minutes longer.
5 Cut 1 or 2 generous slices herb butter for each steak. Top steaks with butter and grill 1 minute longer, or just until butter begins to melt.
6 Transfer steaks to warm plates.

Herb Butter

1 Clove garlic
½ lemon
½ lime
15 g (½ oz) mixed fresh herbs (any combination, including watercress, parsley, dill, basil, marjoram, and rosemary), or 2 level tablespoons dried
125 g (4 oz) unsalted butter, at room temperature

1 Peel and finely chop garlic. Juice enough lemon to measure 2 tablespoons and enough lime to measure 1 tablespoon. Combine juices and remove pits. Wash fresh herbs, if using, pat dry, and chop finely.
2 In food processor or blender, combine butter, garlic, citrus juices, and chopped herbs, and process until well mixed. Or, in medium-size bowl, knead same ingredients together by hand.
3 Form herb butter into log-shaped roll 5 cm (2 inches) long and 5 to 6 cm (2 to 2½ inches) in diameter. Wrap snugly in wax paper and place in freezer for 1 hour or refrigerate for several hours.

Sautéed Spinach with Shallots

750 g to 1 kg (1½ to 2 lbs) young spinach
2 shallots
1 lemon
½ orange
½ lime
4 level tablespoons unsalted butter
Salt
Freshly ground white pepper
4 orange twists (optional)

1 Wash spinach thoroughly, remove stems, and place wet leaves in medium-size bowl. Peel shallots and chop enough to measure 2 tablespoons.
2 Squeeze 60 ml (2 fl oz) lemon juice, 3 to 4 tablespoons orange juice, and 1 tablespoon lime juice. In small bowl, combine juices and remove pits.
3 In large skillet heat butter over medium-high heat until foamy. Add shallots and toss lightly with wooden spatula for 1 minute, removing skillet from heat to keep shallots from burning if necessary.
4 Add spinach and toss to combine thoroughly with butter and shallots.
5 While spinach is still bright green, push to one side of skillet and pour citrus juices into pan. Reduce juices over medium-high heat 30 seconds, then quickly toss spinach with juices and salt and pepper to taste.
6 Serve alongside swordfish steaks and, if desired, garnish each serving with an orange twist.

New Potatoes Braised in Broth with Leeks

750 g (1½ lbs) new red potatoes
250-300 ml (8-10 fl oz) chicken stock
125 ml (4 fl oz) dry white wine
2 tablespoons coarse mustard
Medium-size leek
4 level tablespoons unsalted butter
Salt
Freshly ground pepper

1 Wash potatoes but do not peel. Cut into quarters.
2 In large skillet, combine stock, wine, and mustard. Bring to a boil over medium-high heat, then reduce to a simmer.
3 Trim off root ends and upper leaves of leek, leaving some green, and split leek lengthwise. Gently spread leaves and rinse under cold running water, to remove any sand and grit. Pat dry with paper towel. With chef's knife, cut into 5 mm (½ inch) slices.
4 Add potatoes to simmering broth. Cover and simmer 5 to 7 minutes.
5 In medium-size skillet melt butter over medium-low heat. Add leek and, stirring with wooden spoon, sauteé 8 to 10 minutes.
6 Remove cover from potatoes and simmer uncovered 4 to 5 minutes.
7 Add leeks to potatoes, using rubber spatula to scrape out butter. Cook uncovered 5 minutes, turning occasionally, until broth is reduced and buttery leeks glaze the potatoes. Sprinkle with salt and pepper to taste.
8 With slotted spoon, transfer to dinner plates.

Patricia Unterman

Menu 1
(*Left*)
Avacado and Grapefruit Salad
with Walnut Oil Dressing
Creole Fish and Oyster Stew
Baked Rice with Almonds

Californian Patricia Unterman comes from a family that loves to cook and to eat. Her mother taught her that food should be simple and the basic ingredients of the highest quality. At the San Francisco restaurant that she owns and runs with a partner, Patricia Unterman bases all her cooking on these two principles: 'My partner and I founded the restaurant on the premise that the freshest ingredients need minimal preparation to improve them,' she says.

She favours unusual varieties of fresh fish, which she most often grills over a wood fire and serves with a quickly made sauce; her recipes are flexible, so that a home cook can substitute whatever fish is freshest. She suggests several alternate choices in each menu.

She deals with vegetables in the same spirit, selecting the freshest and seasoning them lightly, as with the Swiss chard with butter and garlic, and the new potatoes with olive oil and basil of Menu 3. Menu 1 and Menu 2 feature salads tossed with delicately flavoured vinaigrettes.

This informal meal features a Creole fish and oyster stew served in large soup bowls. Serve the almond-studded rice separately. Carefully arrange the avacado and grapefruit sections on a bed of watercress and lettuce leaves.

Avocado and Grapefruit Salad with Walnut Oil Dressing
Creole Fish and Oyster Stew
Baked Rice with Almonds

Many varieties of fish will combine well for this spicy stew. If you are using a firm-textured fish like swordfish, pompano, cod, or salmon, add it to the stew earlier than you would a more delicate fish, such as sole or halibut, for longer cooking. Oysters should always go in last, and simmer just until their edges begin to curl.

If you decide to use the optional fresh jalapeño pepper – a small fiery Mexican chili – sample it first for hotness: Slice it in half and taste a piece of it. If it is very hot, use just half of the pepper. However, if you like red-hot food, use the whole pepper, finely minced.

What to drink

This menu demands a wine with enough body to accompany the fish and enough flavour not to disappear in the face of the spices. A California or Alsatian Gewürztraminer will fill the bill.

Start-to-Finish Steps

1 Follow salad recipe steps 1 to 5.
2 Follow fish stew recipe steps 1 and 2.
3 Follow rice recipe steps 1 to 3.

4 Follow fish stew recipe steps 3 to 6.
5 Follow rice recipe steps 4 and 5.
6 While rice is cooking, follow salad recipe step 6 and serve.
7 Follow fish stew recipe steps 7 and 8, and serve with rice.

Avocado and Grapefruit Salad with Walnut Oil Dressing

2 grapefruits (yellow or pink)
2 medium-size ripe avocados
1 shallot
Large bunch watercress
1 head red-leaf lettuce
60 ml (2 fl oz) sherry vinegar
1/2 teaspoon salt
Freshly ground black pepper
60 ml (2 fl oz) walnut oil

1 With paring knife, peel grapefruit, removing all the white pith. Holding the peeled grapefruit over medium-size bowl to catch juice, cut between section membranes to remove any juice. Discard membranes.
2 With paring knife, peel avocados and cut in half lengthwise. Twist halves apart and remove pit. Slice halves lengthwise and add to bowl. With wooden spoon, toss very gently to coat with juice.
3 With chef's knife, peel shallot and chop finely. Trim watercress stems. Remove outer leaves from lettuce and reserve for another use.
4 Wash watercress and lettuce, and dry in salad spinner or pat dry with paper towels. Place in salad bowl, cover, and refrigerate.
5 In small bowl, combine shallot, vinegar, and salt and pepper to taste. Add half of juice from bowl with grapefruit and avocados. In a slow, steady stream, add walnut oil, whisking vigorously until combined.
6 Remove salad bowl from refrigerator. Add half of dressing to watercress and lettuce, and toss until greens are lightly coated. Taste for seasoning. Arrange alternating slices of avocado and grapefruit on top of greens and drizzle with remaining dressing.

28

Creole Fish and Oyster Stew

Medium-size red bell pepper
Medium-size green bell pepper
6 shallots
2 cloves garlic
2 inner stalks celery
1½ teaspoons fresh oregano, or ¾ teaspoon dried
1 fresh jalapeño or serrano chili pepper (optional)
6 level tablespoons unsalted butter
350 ml (12 fl oz) half-and-half milk and cream
250 ml (8 fl oz) fish stock or clam juice
¾ teaspoon paprika
½ teaspoon curry powder
¼ teaspoon cumin
½ teaspoon salt
¼ teaspoon freshly ground white pepper
Cayene pepper
500 g (1 lb) salmon fillet (if available)
500 g (1 lb) of fillets of halibut, petrale sole,
    pompano, swordfish, or cod, plus 1 additional
    pound if not using salmon
12 to 16 shucked oysters with liquor

1 Rinse bell peppers, pat dry with paper towels, core, and seed. Peel shallots and garlic. Wash and trim celery.
2 With chef's knife, mince garlic and finely chop bell peppers, shallots, and celery. Set aside. Wash, dry, and chop fresh oregano, if using. Wearing thin rubber gloves, rinse and seed chili pepper, if using. Finely chop and set aside.
3 In large heavy-gauge skillet melt butter over medium heat. Add bell peppers, shallots, and celery, and sauté until tender, 8 to 10 minutes.
4 Add garlic and oregano to skillet, and cook 30 seconds.
5 Add half-and-half and fish stock or clam juice and bring to a simmer over medium-high heat. Add chili pepper, if using, and paprika, curry powder, cumin, salt, white pepper, and Cayenne to taste, stirring to combine.
6 While fish stock is simmering, wipe fish fillets with damp paper towels. With chef's knife, cut fish into 2½ cm (1 inch) pieces.
7 Add fish to skillet, adding halibut or petrale sole if using, after 1 minute. Return liquid to a simmer, and simmer just until fish is firm, 4 to 5 minutes.
8 Add oysters and liquor, and simmer just until edges of oysters start to curl, about 30 seconds. Check seasoning and ladle into individual soup bowls.

Baked Rice with Almonds

1 teaspoon salt
½ medium-size onion
2 level tablespoons unsalted butter
60 g (2 oz) slivered almonds
175 g (6 oz) long-grain white rice

1 Preheat oven to 190°C (375°F or Mark 5).
2 In medium-size covered saucepan, bring 500 ml (1 pt) water and salt to a boil over high heat.
3 With chef's knife, peel and finely chop onion.
4 In flameproof casserole, melt butter over medium heat. Add onion and almonds, and sauté, stirring with wooden spatula, until onion is translucent and almonds are lightly browned, 3 to 5 minutes.
5 Add rice and stir until coated with butter. Pour in boiling water, stir and bake, covered, until rice has absorbed all water and is tender but still firm, about 18 minutes.

29

Fish Baked in Parchment with Red Peppers
Polenta with Butter and Cheese
Marinated Salad

Fish baked in parchment with julienned red peppers is the focal point of this light meal. Garnish each serving of polenta with a sprig of watercress. The marinated salad, arranged on lettuce leaves, is served on individual plates.

Baking fish in kitchen parchment seals in the fish juices and gently steeps the fish in herbs and seasonings to create a flavourful sauce. If you cannot find parchment, substitute aluminium foil.

Polenta, or cornmeal mush, is a staple in northern Italy. This version calls for you to cook the polenta in a double boiler, stirring it frequently. It will become very stiff, so that when you turn the mixture onto a buttered board and flatten it, it will cool and harden enough to slice.

The marinated salad can accommodate any number of seasonal vegetables, but the mushrooms and black beans should be constant ingredients. As possible alternatives to the cucumbers, Patricia Unterman suggests blanched courgettes or cooked artichoke hearts. The balsamic vinegar in the dressing is a slightly sweet Italian red wine vinegar that is aged in barrels. If you cannot find it, substitute a good-quality red wine vinegar.

What to drink

An Italian wine is the best choice – either a crisp Verdichio or the softer, fruitier Italian Chardonnay.

Start-to-Finish Steps

1 Follow salad recipe step 1.
2 While beans are cooking, folow polenta recipe steps 1 to 5.
3 While polenta is cooking, follow salad recipe steps 2 to 8.
4 Follow fish recipe steps 1 to 9.
5 While fish is baking, follow salad recipe steps 9 to 11.
6 Follow polenta recipe steps 6 to 8.
7 Follow fish recipe steps 10 and 11, polenta recipe 9, and serve with marinated salad.

Fish Baked in Parchment with Red Peppers

Four 2½ cm (1 inch) thick fillets of tuna, halibut, sea bass, salmon, or haddock (each about 250 g (8 oz))
4 red bell peppers (about 625 g (1¼ lb) total weight)
60 ml (2 fl oz) virgin oil
4 cloves garlic
1 level tablespoon chopped fresh oregano, or 1 teaspoon dried
Salt and freshly ground pepper
Medium-size red onion
1 fresh jalapeño or serrano chili pepper (optional)
2 level tablespoons unsalted butter

1 With damp paper towels, wipe fish fillets and set aside.

2 Core, seed, and halve red peppers. Cut lengthwise into 5 mm (¼ inch) wide julienne strips. Peel and mince garlic.

3 In medium-size skillet, heat olive oil over high heat for 1 minute. Reduce heat to medium, add red peppers, and sauté, stirring with wooden spatula, until tender, about 8 minutes. Add garlic, oregano, salt and pepper to taste, and cook 30 seconds, stirring with wooden spatula. Remove pan from heat and set aside.

4 Peel red onion. With chef's knife, cut in half lengthwise, then cut crosswise into paper-thin slices.

5 Wearing thin rubber gloves, rinse chili pepper if using, and dry with paper towel. With paring knife, cut open pepper, and remove seeds with tip of blade. With chef's knife, mince chili.

6 Preheat oven to 230°C (450°F or Mark 8).

7 Cut four 30 by 40 cm (12 by 16 inch) pieces of baking parchment or heavy-duty aluminium foil. Place 1 fillet in centre of each piece. Season each fillet with salt and pepper to taste and top with 2 or 3 slices of onion, one quarter of sautéed red pepper strips, and one quarter of minced chili pepper, if using. Dot each fillet with ½ tablespoon butter.

8 Fold parchment or foil over fillets and seal by folding over edges.

9 Place packages on cookie sheet and bake 8 minutes.

10 Warm dinner plates under hot running water and dry.

11 Remove fish from oven. Slit packets open and slide fish and juices out onto warm plates.

Polenta with Butter and Cheese

125 g (4 oz) yellow cornmeal
1 teaspoon salt
250 g (8 oz) unsalted butter (at room temperature), approximately
125 g (¼ lb) Parmesan cheese
Watercress sprigs for garnish (optional)

1 Bring water to a simmer in bottom of double boiler unit. In large saucepan, bring 625 ml (1¼ pts) of water to a boil, then reduce to a simmer.

2 In medium-size bowl, combine cornmeal, salt, and 350 ml (12 fl oz) cold water, stirring with wooden spoon. To the simmering water, add cornmeal mixture all at once, stirring and flattening any lumps with back of spoon.

3 Immediately transfer cornmeal mixture to top of double boiler and cook over simmering water, stirring frequently, until polenta is thick enough to hold spoon upright, 45 minutes.

4 Grate enough Parmesan cheese to measure 60 g (2 oz).

5 Wash, pat dry, and trim watercress sprigs, if using.

6 Butter a large cutting board or cover 45 cm (18 inch) square section of counter with buttered wax paper.

7 Remove polenta from heat. Using wooden spoon, stir in butter, 2 tablespoons at a time, until thoroughly incorporated. Add cheese and stir until blended.

8 Transfer polenta to buttered board or wax paper. Shape into 30 by 35 by $2^{1}/_{2}$ cm (12 by 14 by 1 inch) rectangle. Let rest 1 minute.

9 With chef's knife, cut into 4 equal pieces. With metal spatula, transfer to dinner plates and garnish with watercress sprigs, if desired.

Marinated Salad

Small onion
100 g (3 oz) dried black beans
60 ml (2 fl oz) balsamic vinegar
Salt
Freshly ground pepper
125 ml (4 fl oz) virgin olive oil
250 g ($^{1}/_{2}$ lb) mushrooms
250 g ($^{1}/_{2}$ lb) broccoli
250 g (8 oz) cherry tomatoes
Medium-size cucumber
4 to 8 large, light green lettuce leaves

1 Peel onion, but do not slice. In small saucepan, cover black beans with 10 cm (4 inches) of cold water. Add onion and bring to a boil over medium-high heat. Reduce heat and simmer 40 to 50 minutes, or until beans are *al dente*.

2 In small bowl, combine vinegar with salt and pepper to taste. In a slow steady stream, add oil, whisking vigorously until combined.

3 Wipe mushrooms clean with damp paper towels. With paring knife, cut mushrooms into 5 mm ($^{1}/_{4}$

inch) slices and place in large bowl. Pour in half the salad dressing and toss mushrooms to coat.

4 In medium-size saucepan over medium-high heat, bring $1^{1}/_{2}$ ltrs ($2^{1}/_{2}$ pts) water to a boil.

5 Wash broccoli and cut into florets. Add to boiling water and cook just until tender, 3 to 5 minutes.

6 Rinse cherry tomatoes and pat dry with paper towels. With chef's knife, slice in half vertically.

7 Using vegetable peeler, peel cucumber. Cut cucumber in half lengthwise. Using spoon, scoop out seeds and discard. Cut cucumber into 5 mm ($^{1}/_{4}$ inch) crescents.

8 In colander, drain broccoli and refresh under cold running water. Pat dry with paper towels and trim off stems on diagonal.

9 In colander, drain black beans, shaking colander gently to drain off liquid. Discard onion.

10 To large bowl with mushrooms, add black beans, broccoli, tomatoes, and cucumber, and toss to combine. Add remaining dressing and toss.

11 Rinse lettuce and dry in salad spinner or pat dry with paper towels. Divide lettuce among 4 individual salad bowls and top each with salad.

Added touch
These rich, buttery coconut cookies, sprinkled with confectioners' sugar, could be complemented by a creamy fruit-flavoured spumoni (an Italian ice cream).

Coconut Butter Cookies

250 g (8 oz) unsalted butter
125 g (4 oz) confectioners' sugar, approximately
250 g (8 oz) flour
$^{1}/_{4}$ teaspoon salt
1 teaspoon vanilla extract
125 g (4 oz) grated moist coconut, fresh or packaged

1 Cut butter into tablespoon-size pieces.

2 In large mixing bowl, using electric mixer at high speed, combine butter and 125 g (4 oz) sugar until completely blended. Reduce speed to low. Add flour, salt, and vanilla, and continue beating until well-blended. Add coconut and blend.

3 Form dough into 2 long rolls about 4 cm ($1^{1}/_{2}$ inches) in diameter and wrap in wax paper. Chill at least 2 hours.

4 Preheat oven to 180°C (350°F or Mark 4).

5 Cut rolls into 5 mm ($^{1}/_{4}$ inch) thick rounds and place $2^{1}/_{2}$ cm (1 inch) apart on cookie sheet. Bake until lightly browned, about 15 minutes.

6 With metal spatula, transfer hot cookies to wire rack to cool. While cookies are warm, shake confectioners' sugar through sieve held over cookies.

Fresh Tomato and Fennel Soup
Trout Baked in Course Salt/Chard in Butter and Garlic
New Potatoes with Basil

When you serve this informal meal, bring the soup to the table in a tureen. Arrange the salt-baked trout on a bed of coarse salt on a large oval platter. The potatoes and the chard come in separate serving dishes.

The ancient Chinese probably devised this technique of cooking food packed in salt. One advantage of this method is the brief cooking time: at high heat, the salt seals in the food, trapping moisture and flavour. The salt does not flavour the trout, which emerges from the salt delicately cooked in its own juices.

Swiss chard is not Swiss at all, but a native of the Mediterranean area. Related to beetroot, chard is esteemed for its earthy, spinach-like taste. Its dark green leaves cook just like spinach, too; the white stems, which are left over in this recipe, cook like celery or asparagus. Select chard that has fresh crisp leaves without any signs of wilting or discolouration. Refrigerate unwashed chard in a plastic bag, where it will last for three to five days.

Use fresh basil or any other fresh herb on the potatoes, but chop it at the last minute to prevent wilting. The potatoes themselves should be tiny and sweet, preferably part of a spring crop.

What to drink
The vivid flavours of this menu require a dry, fruity wine, such as an Italian Pinot Grigio or Pinot Bianco.

Start-to-Finish Steps
1 Follow soup recipe steps 1 and 2.
2 While onion is cooking, follow chard recipe steps 1 and 2, and fish recipe steps 1 and 2.
3 Follow soup recipe step 3.
4 While soup is simmering, follow chard recipe step 3 and potatoes recipe steps 1 and 2.
5 Follow fish recipe step 3 and chard recipe step 4.
6 Follow soup recipe step 4, potatoes recipe step 3.
7 Follow soup recipe steps 5 and 6. While heating soup, follow fish recipe step 5 and potatoes recipe steps 7 and 8, and serve.
8 Follow soup recipe steps 7 and 8, and serve.
9 Follow potatoes recipe step 5 and chard recipe step 5.
10 Follow fish recipe steps 6 and 7, and chard recipe step 6.
11 Follow fish recipe step 8, potatoes recipe step 6, and serve with chard.

Fresh Tomato and Fennel Soup

6 medium-size tomatoes (about 2 kg (3¾ lb) total weight)
Large onion
Small fennel bulb (about 250 g (8 oz), or 1 heaped tablespoon fennel seeds
4 level tablespoons unsalted butter
250 ml (8 fl oz) chicken stock
1 teaspoon salt
Freshly ground pepper
125 ml (4 fl oz) milk

1 Rinse, core, and coarsely chop tomatoes. Peel and slice onion. If using fresh fennel, rinse bulb and slice thinly, reserving sprigs for garnish, if desired.
2 In medium-size saucepan melt butter over medium heat. Add sliced onion and cook, stirring with wooden spatula, until wilted, about 8 minutes.
3 Add tomatoes, fennel or fennel seeds, stock , salt, and pepper to taste. Cover and bring to a boil over high heat. Reduce heat and simmer until fennel is tender, about 20 minutes.
4 Remove from heat and cool 5 minutes.
5 Using ladle, transfer mixture in small batches to food processor or blender, process until smooth, and transfer to large bowl. Rinse saucepan. Place sieve over saucepan and, using back of spoon, push mixture through sieve into saucepan.
6 Add milk to soup and bring to a simmer over medium-high heat.
7 Heat tureen under hot running water and dry.
8 Check and correct seasoning. Ladle soup into tureen and serve.

Trout Baked in Course Salt

2½ kg (5 lbs) coarse (kosher) salt
4 whole trout or red snapper (each about 250 g (8 oz), cleaned and gutted
60 ml (2 fl oz) extra-virgin olive oil
Parsley sprigs for garnish (optional)

1 Cover bottom of 38 by 43 cm (15 by 17 inch) shallow baking pan with 1¾ kg (3½ lbs) coarse salt.
2 Wash fish and pat dry with paper towels.
3 Preheat oven to 250°C (475°F or Mark 9).
4 Place baking pan in oven.
5 Remove pan from oven and arrange fish on hot salt, ensuring that they are not touching. Cover fish

completely with remaining salt. Bake 15 minutes.

6 Heat platter under hot running water and dry.

7 Remove fish from oven and crack off top salt. Gently lift fish out with 2 metal spatulas and place on warmed platter. With pastry brush, remove discoloured salt from top of fish and from belly cavity.

8 Discard discoloured salt in baking pan and transfer remaining salt to another platter. With 2 spatulas, transfer fish onto bed of salt. Drizzle olive oil over fish and garnish with parsley sprigs, if desired.

Chard in Butter and Garlic

3 bunches red or green chard (about 1³/₄ kg (3¹/₂ lbs) total weight)
6 level tablespoons unsalted butter
1 clove garlic
Salt
Freshly ground pepper
1 lemon

1 In large covered saucepan, bring 2¹/₂ ltrs (4 pts) water and 2 teaspoons salt to a boil over high heat.

2 Trim green chard leaves from central stems, reserving stems for another use. Rinse leaves and shake off excess water.

3 Drop leaves into boiling water and cook just until tender, 5 to 7 minutes.

4 In colander, drain chard, refresh under cold running water and, with wooden spoon, press out extra liquid.

5 In same saucepan, melt butter over medium heat. Peel garlic and put through garlic press or mince finely. Sauté in butter about 1 minute.

6 Add chard and salt and pepper to taste, and squeeze in lemon juice to taste. With wooden spoon or spatula, toss gently to mix and sauté until heated through, 2 to 3 minutes. Transfer to serving plate.

New Potatoes with Basil

12 small new red potatoes, each about 4 cm (1¹/₂ inches) in diameter (about 750 g (1¹/₂ lbs) total weight)
8 fresh basil leaves
3 tablespoons extra-virgin olive oil
Salt
Freshly ground pepper

1 Wash potatoes and drain in colander.

2 Wash basil leaves and pat dry with paper towels.

Using paring knife, cut basil into fine strips, 1 to 3 mm (¹/₁₆ to ¹/₈ inch) thick.

3 In medium-size saucepan bring 2 ltrs (3 pts) water to a boil over high heat.

4 Add potatoes to boiling water. Reduce heat to medium and simmer, covered, until fork pierces potatoes easily, 10 to 15 minutes.

5 In colander, drain potatoes. Halve potatoes, return to saucepan, and cover.

6 Uncover pan, add oil, basil, and salt and pepper to taste, and toss with 2 wooden spoons. Transfer to serving bowl.

Added touch
This light, fudgy cake will have a cracked top. Be careful not to overbake it; the cake should be moist.

Carlo's Chocolate Earthquake Cake

350 g (³/₄ lb) semi-sweet chocolate
125 g (4 oz) unsalted butter
4 eggs, at room temperature
350 g (12 oz) confectioners' sugar
60 g (2 oz) potato flour or plain flour
2 tablespoons grated orange rind
1 teaspoon vanilla extract

1 Preheat oven to 180°C (350°F or Mark 4).

2 In top of double boiler, combine chocolate and butter. Place over almost simmering water and stir until just melted, 4 to 5 minutes. With rubber spatula, scrape into medium-size bowl and let cool slightly.

3 Generously butter and flour 20 cm (8 inch) round cake pan. Cut round of baking parchment or wax paper and cover bottom of pan.

4 Wash upper half of double boiler and crack eggs into it. Place over simmering water and, with electric mixer at high speed, beat until approximately double in volume and eggs are light-coloured, creamy, and form soft peaks, 10 to 15 minutes.

5 Sift sugar and then sift sugar together with flour.

6 Pour chocolate mixture into egg mixture and, with wooden spoon, stir gently to combine. Add sugar and flour mixture, one third at a time, stirring well with metal spoon after each addition. Stir in orange rind and vanilla extract.

7 Pour batter into prepared cake pan, place in oven, and bake 30 minutes. Let cool before removing from pan. Cake will have texture of a light, very fudgy brownie.

Josephine Araldo

Menu 1
(*Right*)
Quenelles with Shallot Sauce
Potatoes with Onions and Cheese
Sautéed Carrots and Grapes

A star pupil of Cordon Bleu chef Henri-Paul Pellaprat, Josephine Araldo nonetheless attributes her imaginative combinations of fruits and vegetables to her grandmother, who not only taught young Josephine to cook but to respect fresh food. In fact, all the vegetable recipes in these three menus were inspired by her grandmother. The most unusual combination, and a favourite of Josephine Araldo's, is carrots with grapes that accompany the quenelles and potatoes in Menu 1.

From her grandmother she also learned kitchen economy, and she believes that a sign of a truly good cook is the ability to work creatively with leftovers. The fish and the vegetable recipes of Menu 2 typify her waste-not philosophy. The cooking liquid for the sole fillets is the base for its flavourful sauce, and the sliced courgettes are cooked in and served with the same herb- and wine-enriched stock.

A master of haute cuisine (she was crowned with her white chef's toque by M. Pellaprat himself), she nonetheless describes herself as a practical cook who uses simple tools and basic techniques, fish being a favourite food because it requires so little treatment. She also sings while while she cooks. 'Singing makes you cook better,' she says. She shops early every day to select quality foods at the best price. She avoids using costly ingredients when less expensive ones will do. For instance, in Menu 3 she features whiting, an ordinary fish often considered inelegant. Here, served with a delicate lemon sauce and accompanied by lima bean soup and a side dish of cucumbers and Brussels sprouts flavoured with gin or juniper berries, the whiting becomes a company meal.

Formal dinnerware underlines the elegance of quenelles served with a creamy herb sauce. Browned sliced potatoes with onions and cheese and sliced carrots with grapes are perfect partners.

Quenelles with Shallot Sauce
Potatoes with Onions and Cheese
Sautéed Carrots and Grapes

You cannot make quenelles – classic French fish dumplings – without a food processor, which shortens the otherwise lengthy preparation time to minutes. A blender is not a substitute because its blades will clog with the fish flesh. Then fish paste must be packed in ice to be firm enough to absorb the cream before poaching. Quenelles are cooked when they float to the surface.

What to drink
A Graves or an Entre-Duex-Mers, both medium-bodied, flavourful wines, would be good with the quenelles.

Start-to-Finish Steps
1 Follow quenelles recipe steps 1 to 3.
2 Follow potatoes recipe steps 1 to 7.
3 Prepare herbs for quenelles and sauce. Follow quenelles recipes steps 4 to 8.
4 Follow sauce recipe steps 1 and 2.
5 Follow carrots recipe steps 1 and 2.
6 Follow quenelles recipe steps 9 to 13. While first batch of quenelles is poaching, follow carrots recipe step 3. While second batch is poaching, follow carrots recipe step 4 and potatoes recipe step 8. While third batch is poaching, follow sauce recipe step 3, and while fourth batch is poaching, follow sauce recipe step 4.
7 Follow potatoes recipe step 9, and lower heat to SLOW, leaving oven door ajar for 1 minute.
8 Place quenelles in oven, step 14.
9 Place carrots recipe step 5, sauce recipe step 5, quenelles recipe step 15, and serve with potatoes.

Quenelles with Shallot Sauce

350 g (³/₄ lb) sea or bay scallops
350 g (³/₄ lb) fillets of sole
350-500 ml (12-16 fl oz) heavy cream
Salt
¹/₂ tablespoon finely minced shallot
1 clove garlic, peeled and finely minced
¹/₄ teaspoon freshly ground white pepper
1 egg
1 tablespoon Cognac
2 level tablespoons chopped parsley
Shallot sauce (see following recipe)

1 In colander, rinse scallops. Pat dry with paper towels.
2 Wipe fillets with damp paper towels. With chef's knife, cut each fillet crosswise into thirds.
3 Combine scallops and sole in bowl of food processor, cover, and place in freezer to chill at least 15 minutes. Place cream and large mixing bowl in refrigerator to chill.
4 Remove food processor bowl from freezer, add ¹/₂ teaspoon salt, and process fish until thick and smooth.
5 Set chilled mixing bowl in another slightly larger bowl filled with ice. Scrape fish mixture into bowl. Add shallot, garlic, salt, and pepper, and beat until blended.
6 In small bowl, beat egg with fork. Add egg to fish mixture and beat until blended.
7 Add cream to fish mixture 60 ml (2 fl oz) at a time, beating after each addition until totally incorporated. Stop adding cream when fish mixture is thick and stiff.
8 Add Cognac and parsley, and beat until blended. Cover bowl and chill until ready to proceed.
9 In large skillet, bring 5 cm (2 inches) of water and 1 teaspoon salt to a boil.
10 While water is coming to a boil, line shallow roasting pan with aluminium foil and line platter with paper towels. Fill a glass with cold water and in it place 2 tablespoons, bowls down. Remove fish mixture from refrigerator. Adjust heat under skillet so that water barely shivers.
11 Remove tablespoons from glass. With one spoon, pick up a rounded spoonful of fish mixture and smooth the top with the back of the other. Then, with the second spoon, nudge the quenelle off the first spoon into the skillet. Working quickly, repeat, always rewetting the spoons, until about one quarter of the mixture has been used. You should have 10 to 12 quenelles. (As you add quenelles, adjust heat to keep water at the barest simmer, being careful not to let it boil.) Poach quenelles 2 to 3 minutes.
12 With slotted spoon, transfer quenelles to paper-towel-lined platter and then to roasting pan. Cover roasting pan loosely with foil and keep warm on stove top.
13 Repeat procedure threee more times.
14 When all quenelles have been cooked, place

roasting pan in SLOW oven until ready to serve.

15 When ready to serve, remove quenelles from oven, divide among 4 dinnerplates, and top with sauce.

Shallot Sauce

3 level tablespoons unsalted butter
2 level tablespoons finely minced shallots
250 ml (8 fl oz) dry Sauterne
125 ml (4 fl oz) fish stock or clam juice
1/4 teaspoon freshly ground white pepper
2 level tablespoons flour
2 level tablespoons chopped dill
2 level tablespoons chopped parsley
1 to 2 tablespoons heavy cream

1 In small saucepan, melt 1 level tablespoon butter over medium heat. Add shallots and sauté 2 minutes.

2 Slowly stir in Sauterne. Raise heat to medium-high and reduce liquid by half, about 5 minutes. Add fish stock and pepper, and stir to combine. Reduce heat to medium.

3 In small bowl, cream remaining butter with back of spoon until soft. Add flour and blend until totally incorporated to form *buerre manié*.

4 Add *buerre manié* to sauce 1 teaspoon at a time, whisking after each addition until blended before adding more. Simmer 2 minutes and keep warm over very low heat.

5 Just before serving, stir in dill, parsley and cream.

Potatoes with Onions and Cheese

4 medium-size potatoes (about 750 g (1 1/2 lbs) total weight)
250 ml (8 fl oz) chicken stock, approximately
2 medium-size onions
2 to 3 level tablespoons unsalted butter
125 g (1/4 lb) Swiss cheese, thinly sliced
Salt and freshly ground white pepper

1 Preheat oven to 190°C (375°F or Mark 5).

2 Fill large bowl with cold water. Peel potatoes and drop them in bowl as you peel them.

3 With chef's knife, cut potatoes into 2 1/2 mm (1/8 inch) slices.

4 In small saucepan, heat stock over medium heat.

5 Peel and chop onions. In medium-size skillet, melt butter over medium heat. Add onions and sauté 2 minutes.

6 Meanwhile, butter ovenproof baking dish.

7 In baking dish, layer potatoes, onions, and cheese, adding salt and pepper to taste after you form each layer, and ending with cheese on top. Pour in enough hot stock to fill dish three quarters full. Cover dish with aluminium foil and bake 30 minutes.

8 Uncover potatoes, and bake 10 minutes longer, or until brown crust has formed.

9 Remove potatoes from oven; keep warm on stove top.

Sautéed Carrots and Grapes

250 g (1/2 lb) seedless grapes, preferably red
1 kg (2 lbs) carrots
4 level tablespoons unsalted butter
175 ml (6 fl oz) chicken stock
Salt and freshly ground white pepper
1 level tablespoon sugar
1 level tablespoon chopped fresh mint
1 teaspoon chopped fresh parsley

1 Remove stems from grapes. In colander, rinse grapes and drain. Pat dry with paper towels and set aside.

2 Peel carrots and cut into 1 cm (1/2 inch) rounds.

3 In medium-size saucepan, melt 3 level tablespoons butter over medium-high heat. Add carrots and sauté 1 minute.

4 Stir in stock and salt and pepper to taste. Raise heat to high and bring to a boil. Reduce heat to low and cook carrots, covered, 10 minutes or just until tender.

5 Remove pan from heat. Add grapes and sugar, and stir gently to combine. Stir in remaining tablespoon butter, mint, and parsley. Divide among four dinner plates.

Avocado and Potato Soup
Fillets of Sole in Wine Sauce
Courgette Merveille

For this meal, sole fillets bake in a glass dish with chopped onion, carrot, and herbs, all of which enhance the mild flavour of the fish. Cover the fillets with a layer of buttered wax paper, then with a layer of foil to prevent the sole from discolouring.

Although there are numerous varieties of avocados, most taste very much alike. For the soup, select avocados that yield to slight pressure and are free of blemishes. To ripen an avocado, place it in a paper bag and leave it at room temperature. Test for ripeness by inserting a toothpick or slender skewer into the avocado at its stem end. The avocado is ripe if the toothpick moves easily. Once ripened, avocados should be refrigerated.

What to drink
For a change of pace, try a young Spanish white wine from the Rioja district. A California Pinot Blanc would also go well with this meal.

Start-to-Finish Steps
1 Follow soup recipe steps 1 to 3.
2 While potatoes are cooking, follow courgette recipe steps 1 to 4.
3 Chop chives for soup recipe and prepare vegetables and herbs for sole recipe.
4 Follow sole recipe step 1.
5 Follow soup recipe steps 4 to 7.
6 Follow courgette recipe step 5 and sole recipe steps 2 and 3.
7 While sole is baking, follow courgette recipe step 6.
8 Follow sole recipe steps 4 and 5 and soup recipe steps 8 and 9.
9 Follow sole recipe steps 6 and 7, soup recipe step 10, and serve with courgettes.

Mugs of creamy avocado soup, garnished with slices of ripe avocado and chopped chives, introduce this simple meal: fillets of sole in wine sauce and a colourful medley of gently cooked fresh vegetables.

Avocado and Potato Soup

4 medium-size potatoes (about 750 g (1½ lbs) total weight)
2 large avocados plus 1 small avocado for garnish (optional)
30 g (1 oz) finely chopped chives plus 2 teaspoons chopped chives for garnish (optional)
750 ml (1½ pts) chicken stock
125 ml (4 fl oz) dry sherry
Salt
Freshly ground pepper

1   In medium-size saucepan, bring 2½ ltrs (4 pts) of water to a boil over high heat.
2   Fill medium-size bowl with cold water. Peel and quarter potatoes, and drop them in bowl as you peel them.
3   Add potatoes to boiling water, cover, and cook until tender, 15 to 20 minutes, or until potatoes can be pierced easily with tip of knife.
4   In colander, drain potatoes and return to warm pan.
5   Peel 2 large avocados and halve lengthwise, cutting around pit. Twist to separate halves. Remove pit and discard. Cut flesh into chunks and place in bowl of food processor or blender.
6   If using food processor, add potatoes and chives, and process until mashed. If using blender, add potatoes, chives, and 250 ml (8 fl oz) cup of stock, and process until smooth.
7   With rubber spatula, scrape mixture into pan in which potatoes were cooked. Add stock, sherry, and salt and pepper to taste, and stir until blended.
8   Stirring frequently with wooden spoon, bring soup just to a simmer over medium-high heat.
9   While soup is heating, peel, halve, and pit small avocado, if using for garnish. Cut each half lengthwise into four 1 cm (½ inch) thick slices.
10 Divide soup among individual bowls or mugs and, if desired, garnish with avocado slices and remaining chopped chives.

Fillets of Sole in Wine Sauce

Four 1 cm (½ inch) thick fillets of sole (each about 200 g (7 oz))
2 level tablespoons unsalted butter, approximately
125 g (4 oz) chopped onion
60 g (2 oz) chopped carrot
1 level tablespoon chopped fresh thyme, or 1 teaspoon dried
1 level tablespoon chopped fresh fennel
1 level tablespoon snipped fresh dill
1 bay leaf
125 ml (4 fl oz) white wine
Salt
Freshly ground pepper
2 tablespoons flour

1   Preheat oven to 190°C (375°F or Mark 5). Wipe fillets with damp paper towels.
2   Cut a sheet of wax paper to fit baking dish and butter lightly.
3   In heatproof glass baking dish, place onion, carrot, thyme, fennel, dill, and bay leaf. Top vegetables and herbs with fillets. Add wine, 125 ml (4 fl oz) water, and salt and freshly ground pepper to taste. Cover with wax paper, buttered side down. Top with a sheet of aluminium foil and crimp foil around edges of the dish. Bake 12 to 15 minutes or until fish barely flakes when tested with tip of sharp knife.
4   In small bowl, cream 2 level tablespoons butter with back of spoon until soft. Add flour and, with fingers or back of spoon, blend until totally incorporated to form *buerre manié*.
5   Place dinner plates under hot running water to warm.
6   Just before fish is done, dry plates. Remove fish from oven and, with metal spatula, transfer fillets to warm dinner plates. Drain cooking liquid through a fine-mesh sieve set over small saucepan. Add *buerre manié* to pan and whisk until blended, 2 to 3 minutes. Taste for seasoning.
7   Spoon sauce over each fillet.

Courgette Merveille

750 g (1½ lbs) courgettes
12 white boiling onions or 3 large onions
1 clove garlic
2 large tomatoes or 500g (16 oz) can Italian plum tomatoes
1 sprig fresh thyme, or 1 pinch of dried
1 sprig fresh oregano, or 1 pinch dried
1 sprig fresh marjoram, or 1 pinch of dried
1 lemon
2 tablespoons olive oil
250 ml (8 fl oz) chicken stock
250 ml (8 fl oz) white wine
Salt
Freshly ground pepper

1   Fill medium-size saucepan with water to within 5 cm (2 inches) of the rim and bring to a boil over high heat.
2   While water is coming to a boil, wash courgettes,

pat dry with paper towels, and cut on diagonal into 1 cm (1/2 inch) thick slices. Peel onions and, if using large onions, quarter them. Peel and mince garlic.

3   Drop tomatoes into boiling water and let stand 1 minute. With slotted spoon, transfer to colander, and cool under cold running water. Peel and halve, and seed. Cut into quarters. If using canned tomatoes, drain.

4   If using fresh herbs, strip leaves from stems. Grate lemon zest, then slice lemon in half and juice.

5   In large saucepan, heat 2 tablespoons olive oil briefly over medium-high heat. Add onions and garlic, and sauté, stirring frequently with wooden spoon, 4 to 5 minutes.

6   Add tomatoes, stock wine, lemon juice, lemon zest, herbs, and salt and pepper to taste and stir to combine. Bring to a boil and add courgettes. Reduce heat to medium and cook just until courgettes are tender, about 10 minutes. Cover pan partially, remove from heat, and keep warm until ready to serve.

Added touch

This version of chocolate soufflé bakes while you eat dinner or while your guests have after-dinner coffee.

Chocolate Soufflé

2 tablespoons brewed coffee or 1 teaspoon instant freeze-dried granules
4 large eggs, at room temperature
3 level tablespoons unsalted butter, approximately
125 g (4 oz) sugar
Two 30 g (1 oz) squares unsweetened chocolate
30 g (1 oz) plain flour
250 ml (8 fl oz) milk
1 teaspoon vanilla extract
1/4 teaspoon salt
1/4 teaspoon cream of tartar
250 ml (8 fl oz) heavy cream (optional)

1   Reserve 2 tablespoons coffee from your morning cup or, in small saucepan, bring 2 tablespoons water to a boil and add 1 teaspoon instant freeze-dried granules. Set aside.

2   Separate eggs, placing 3 whites in large non-aluminium bowl and 4 yolks in small bowl, and reserving extra white for another use.

3   Lightly butter 1¼ ltr (2 pt) soufflé dish. Sprinkle butter with 2 level tablespoons sugar. Tilt dish on its side and roll it around to distribute sugar evenly.

4   In lower half of double boiler, bring 2½ cm (1 inch) of water to a simmer over medium heat. In upper half of double boiler, combine chocolate and coffee, and set over lower half, stirring occasionally with whisk, until chocolate is melted, 3 to 5 minutes.

5   When chocolate has melted, add butter, 1 tablespoon at a time, whisking after each addition until butter is incorporated before adding more.

6   Add flour and stir until blended. Continue to cook, stirring, 4 to 5 minutes.

7   While flour-chocolate mixture is cooking, scald milk in small saucepan over medium heat bringing it just up to – but not to – the boiling point. Preheat oven to 200°C (400°F or Mark 6).

8   Remove chocolate mixture from heat, but leave lower half of double boiler on burner. Add 60 g (2 oz) plus 1 tablespoon sugar and scalded milk and stir until blended.

9   Return upper half of double boiler to lower half and cook, stirring constantly, until very thick, 7 to 10 minutes. Again remove from heat and beat mixture about 1 minute.

10 Beat in egg yolks, one at a time, until totally incorporated. Beat in vanilla extract.

11 To large bowl with egg whites, add salt. With whisk or electric beater at medium speed, beat whites until foamy. Add cream of tartar and beat whites until soft peaks form. Add remaining tablespoon sugar and continue to beat just until whites stand stiff, shiny peaks. Do not overbeat.

12 With rubber spatula, scoop up one-third of beaten whites and fold into cooled chocolate. Then with spatula carefully fold in remaining whites.

13 Gently turn mixture into prepared soufflé dish, filling dish three quarters full. With knife, make a 1 cm (1/2 inch) deep cut around circumference of batter, 2½ cm (1 inch) in from edge of dish. The crust will break at this point and form a taller centre, creating a top-hat effect when the soufflé has risen.

14 Place soufflé on middle shelf of preheated oven for 3 to 5 minutes, then reduce temperature to 190°C (375°F or Mark 5) and bake an additional 20 minutes.

15 If using whipped cream as an accompaniment, chill mixing bowl and beaters in freezer 15 minutes before soufflé is done. Five minutes before soufflé is done, remove bowl and beaters from refrigerator and pour cream into bowl. Whip at medium speed until cream has thickened but is still soft and a little runny. Turn into serving bowl.

16 Remove soufflé from oven and bring to the table immediately. Using 2 large spoons, serve each diner a portion of the crust and a portion of the interior of the soufflé If using whipped cream, spoon a few tablespoons alongside each serving.

Offer this casual meal buffet style: Set out a tureen of lima bean soup with a bowl of sautéed cucumbers and Brussels sprouts. Arrange the whiting fillets on a platter, and serve the sauce separately.

Whiting, which may flake apart during cooking, requires gentle handling when fried, as in this recipe. The puréed lima bean soup is flavoured with fresh herbs and thickened with *crème fraîche*, a cultured cream with a slightly tart, nutty taste. Once a French speciality, crème fraîche is hard to find ready-made except at gourmet shops and certain supermarkets, but you can make a reasonable facsimile of it yourself.

What to drink

An Italian Soave would be ideal here, or try a dry California Chenin-Blanc – both are soft and medium bodied.

Start-to-Finish Steps

At least 8 hours ahead: If making crème fraîche, combine 125 ml (4 fl oz) sour cream with 250 ml (8 fl oz) heavy cream in jar with lid or in small bowl. Blend thoroughly, cover partially, and set in warm (but not hot) place for about 8 hours or until mixture thickens. Cover and refrigerate. Crème fraîche will keep about 10 days.

1   Follow lima bean soup recipe steps 1 to 3.
2   While lima beans are cooking, prepare herbs for cucumbers and brussels sprouts and follow recipe step 1.
3   If using fresh Brussels sprouts, follow cucumbers and Brussels sprouts recipe step 2.
4   Follow soup recipe step 4.
5   Cut baguette in half, reserving one half for another use. Process enough bread in blender to yield 60 g (2 oz) crumbs.
6   Follow whiting recipe steps 1 to 5.
7   Follow cucumbers recipe steps 3 to 8; if using frozen sprouts, omit steps 5 and 7. Turn off heat.
8   Follow soup recipe steps 5 to 8 and serve.
9   Follow cucumbers recipe step 9.
10 While sprouts are cooking, remove whiting from refrigerator and follow whiting recipe steps 6 to 8.
11 Follow cucumbers recipe step 10, whiting recipe step 9, and serve.

Lima Bean Soup

Small onion
Small carrot
1 level tablespoon unsalted butter
350 ml (12 fl oz) chicken stock
500 g (1 lb) fresh lima beans
1 tablespoon chopped fresh tarragon, or 1 teaspoon dried
1 tablespoon chopped fresh parsley or chervil
Salt and freshly ground pepper
1 egg
100 ml (3 fl oz) crème fraîche

1   Peel and chop onion and carrot.
2   In medium-size saucepan, melt butter over medium heat. Add onion and carrot, and sauté, stirring with wooden spoon, until onion is translucent, 4 to 5 minutes.
3   Add 250 ml (8 fl oz) stock to pan and stir to combine. Raise heat to medium-high and bring to a boil. Add lima beans, return liquid to a boil, and cook beans 5 minutes, or until just tender.
4   Transfer beans and cooking liquid to bowl of food processor or blender. Add tarragon and parsley or chervil, and process until smooth. Return mixture to saucepan. Add remaining stock and salt and pepper to taste, and stir until blended. Rinse processor or blender bowl and dry.
5   Bring soup to a boil, over medium-high heat, stirring frequently. Reduce heat and simmer 5 minutes.
6   While soup simmers, separate egg using 2 small bowls. With fork, beat yolk lightly; reserve white for another use. Add crème fraîche to yolk and stir with fork until blended.
7   Stirring with wooden spoon, pour yolk and crème fraîche mixture into soup and continue to stir until blended.
8   Transfer soup to tureen and serve.

Whiting with Lemon Sauce

250 g (8 oz) unsalted butter, approximately
4 fillets of whiting (silver hake) (about 750 g (1 1/2 lbs) total weight
60 g (2 oz) flour
60 g (2 oz) bread crumbs
2 eggs
1 tablespoon vegetable oil
1 lemon
1/2 teaspoon celery seeds
Pinch of cloves
Salt and freshly ground pepper
Fennel tops for garnish (optional)
Red radish floret for garnish (optional)

1   Place 125 g (4 oz) butter in medium-size bowl and set aside to soften.
2   Wipe fillets with damp paper towels.
3   Place flour and bread crumbs in separate pie pans or on flat plates. Break eggs into shallow bowl and beat with fork. Arrange dishes so that egg is in the middle.
4   One at a time, dip fillets in flour, coating both sides. Gently shake off excess and dip fillet in egg. Let excess drain off and dip fillet in breadcrumbs, coating both sides. Lay breaded fillet on plate. Repeat until all fillets are breaded. Cover with plastic wrap and chill until ready to proceed.
5   Line platter with paper towels.
6   In large heavy-gauge skillet, melt oil and 2 level tablespoons of butter over medium-high heat. Tilt pan back and forth to combine fats. When butter and oil begin to foam, add fillets and lower heat to medium. Cook fillets about 3 minutes per side or until light brown. Add additional butter as necessary, using up to 6 more tablespoons.
7   While fillets are browning, prepare sauce: Juice lemon. Add lemon juice, celery seeds, cloves, and salt and pepper to taste to softened butter, and beat until blended. Transfer sauce to small jug or sauceboat.
8   With metal spatula, transfer fillets to paper-towel-lined platter to drain.
9   Arrange fillets on serving platter and garnish with fennel tops and radish floret, if desired. Serve sauce separately.

Cucumbers and Brussels Sprouts

750 g (1½ lbs) fresh Brussels sprouts, or two 300 g
    (10 oz) packages frozen
Salt
Medium-size onion
2 cucumbers (about 750 g (1½ lbs) total weight)
1 lime
6 or 7 juniper berries, crushed, or 2 to 3 tablespoons
    gin
4 level tablespoons unsalted butter
1 level tablespoon chopped fresh fennel leaves, fresh
    snipped dill, or dill seeds.
1 teaspoon sugar
freshly ground pepper

1 Pick over Brussels sprouts, removing yellow leaves.
   In colander, rinse sprouts under cold running
   water and drain. Set aside.
2 If using fresh Brussels sprouts, fill medium-size
   saucepan with 2½ltrs (4 pts) water, add 2 teaspoons
   salt, and bring to a boil over high heat.
3 Peel onion and chop coarsely.
4 Peel cucumbers and halve lengthwise. Seed
   cucumbers by drawing a teaspoon or melon baller
   down middle of cut side of each cucumber.
   Discard seeds and chop cucumber coarsely.

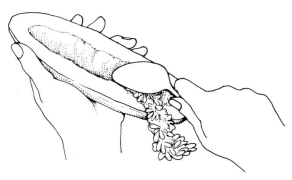

5 Add fresh sprouts to boiling water, return water to
   a boil, reduce to a simmer, and blanch sprouts 5
   minutes.
6 While sprouts are blanching, juice lime and crush
   juniper berries with back of spoon.
7 In colander, drain sprouts and refresh under cold
   running water. Set aside.
8 In large skillet, melt butter over medium heat. Add
   onion and sauté, stirring with wooden spoon, until
   onion is translucent, 4 to 5 minutes.
9 Add cucumbers and blanched or frozen Brussels
   sprouts, and stir to combine. Add chopped fennel
   leaves or dill, juniper berries or gin, lime juice,
   sugar, and salt and pepper to taste. Cover skillet,
   reduce heat to low, and cook 7 to 10 minutes if
   using fresh sprouts, 3 to 5 minutes if using frozen

sprouts, or until vegetables are tender but still *al
dente.*
10 Turn vegetables into serving bowl.

Added touch

For this variation on the French *petits pots de crème,*
you will need small ovenproof dishes.

Breton Coffee Cream

300 ml (10 fl oz) light cream
1½ teaspoons instant coffee
3 eggs
100 g (3 oz) sugar
Pinch of salt
1 teaspoon vanilla extract
125 ml (4 fl oz) heavy cream for garnish (optional)

1 Preheat oven to 180°C (350°F or Mark 4).
2 In large saucepan, over low heat, heat 300 ml (10
   fl oz) light cream. When cream has warmed
   enough to be too hot for your finger, add instant
   coffee and, with metal spoon, stir to blend.
3 Separate eggs. Place yolks in medium-size bowl
   and reserve whites for another use.
4 With electric beater on high, beat yolks until thick
   and lemon-coloured, approximately 5 minutes.
   Gradually add sugar and beat until well-blended
   and smooth. Add salt and beat to combine.
5 Lower beater speed to medium and slowly pour in
   cream, beating constantly, until thoroughly
   combined. Beat in vanilla extract.
6 Put coffee cream through fine-mesh sieve into
   another medium-size bowl, stirring with a spoon
   to help the mixture through the mesh.
7 Spoon the mixture into pots de crème dishes, small
   ramekins, or custard cups, cover with aluminium
   foil, and place ramekins in baking dish.
8 Pull oven shelf part way out and set baking dish
   on it. Carefully pour water around the cups to
   come halfway up sides of cups.
9 Close oven and bake coffee creams for 20 minutes.
   Remove from oven, let cool at room temperature
   for 30 minutes, and then refrigerate, covered, until
   chilled, approximately 1 hour.
10 If serving with optional whipped cream, chill bowl
   and beaters while coffee creams cool.
11 Five minutes before ready to serve, place heavy
   cream in chilled bowl and beat at medium speed
   until thickened but still runny, 4 to 5 minutes (a
   ribbon of cream will leave a trail on surface rather
   than immediately reincorporating into rest of
   cream).
12 Serve coffee creams garnished with whipped
   cream, if desired.

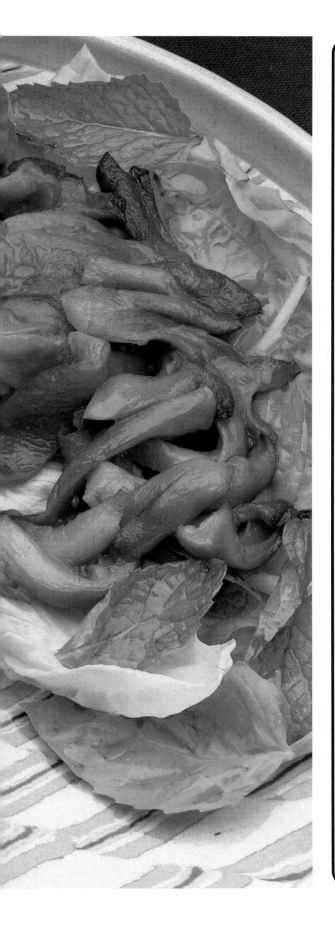

Bruce Cliborne

Menu 1
(*Left*)
Sautéed Scallops
with White Wine Sauce
Spicy Spinach Sauté
Wild Mushroom Salad
with Basil and Mint

Bruce Cliborne spent his childhood summers on his grandparents' farm in rural Virginia, where they grew their own produce and raised their own beef, pork, and chicken. His grandmother's homemade sausages and freshly churned butter are some of the memories that inspire his use of fresh, pure ingredients in cooking.

According to this cook, the culinary arts are analogous to the fine arts. As art students study the masters, begining cooks should study the classic techniques of the world's finest chefs. With this solid grounding, cooks can be inventive. 'Making good food should be challenging, intriguing, amusing, and hard work,' says Bruce Cliborne.

He draws upon the cuisines of France (his major gastronomic influence), Japan, Italy, and China for inspiration, and his meals often contain elements of several, as in the menus here. In Menu 1, fresh basil, a favourite French and Italian herb, seasons the wild mushroom salad. To the French-inspired sautéed scallops, Bruce Cliborne adds hot dried chilies, which are common to Asian cooking. The two Oriental stir-fry dishes of Menu 3 are accompanied by an Italian speciality, fettuccine, with garlic as the unifying flavour for all three recipes.

The mussels and shrimp of Menu 2, an amalgam of European and Asian recipes, combines such diverse ingredients as coconut cream, mint, vermouth, olive oil, and snow peas.

For a festive meal, present scallops on a bed of sautéed spinach garnished with orange zest, and sautéed wild mushrooms on a bed of greens.

Sautéed Scallops with White Wine Sauce
Spicy Spinach Sauté
Wild Mushroom Salad with Basil and Mint

The salad for this company meal requires several unusual ingredients: arugula, lamb's tongue lettuce, and a choice of one of several varieties of fresh wild mushrooms. Arugula is a pungent Italian green that combines well with milder salad greens. Mild lamb's tongue lettuce, also known as *mâche*, grows in clumps of 10 to 15 tongue-shaped leaves. Rinse the greens well in cold water to remove any grit, wrap the clean leaves in paper towels, and refrigerate. Use them within a day or two. You can substitute butter lettuce if you wish. If you cannot locate chanterelles, shiitake, or enokitake, substitute fresh cultivated mushrooms. Note: Unless you are an expert, under no circumstances should you use wild mushrooms picked on your own.

What to drink

A good-quality California Sauvignon Blanc or a good Graves would go well with the rich flavours here.

Start-to-Finish Steps

1 Prepare clarified butter for scallops recipe. You will need 125 g (4 oz) plus 2 tablespoons to yield enough.
2 While butter is melting, mince garlic for spinach recipe, mince shallot for sauce recipe, and slice

shallots for salad recipe. Juice orange for sauce recipe and julienne rind, if using, for scallops recipe. Juice lemons for salad and for scallops.
3 Follow sauce recipe steps 1 to 3.
4 Follow salad recipe steps 1 and spinach recipe step 1.
5 Follow salad recipe steps 1 and 3, and wipe out pan.
6 Follow scallops recipe steps 1 to 7.
7 Follow spinach recipe steps 2 and 3.
8 Follow salad recipe steps 4 and 5, scallops recipe steps 8 and 9, and serve.

Sautéed Scallops with White Wine Sauce

750 g (1½ lbs) plump sea scallops
3 eggs
60 g (2 oz) flour
125 ml (4 fl oz) clarified butter
125 ml (4 fl oz) olive oil
6 whole dried chili peppers
Juice of 1½ lemons
White wine sauce (see following recipe)
1 level tablespoon julienned orange peel for garnish (optional)

1 In colander, rinse scallops under cold running water. Drain and pat dry with paper towels. Preheat oven to SLOW.
2 Separate eggs into small bowls. Reserve whites for another use. Lightly whisk yolks with 2 tablespoons cold water.
3 Place flour on large flat plate.
4 Dip each scallop in yolks, let excess drip off, then roll in flour, coating evenly. Gently shake off excess flour.
5 In large sauté pan, heat 60 ml (2 fl oz) clarified butter and 60 ml (2 fl oz) olive oil over medium-high heat.
6 When butter-oil mixture is hot, add 3 chili peppers to pan. Cook, stirring with wooden spatula, until peppers begin to brown, 3 to 4 minutes. Using slotted spoon, remove peppers from pan and discard.
7 Add half the scallops to the pan and sauté until

golden, about 3 minutes per side. With slotted spoon, transfer scallops to paper-towel-lined heatproof platter and keep warm in oven. Repeat with remaining chilies, adding more butter and oil as necessary, for second batch of scallops.

8   Remove scallops from oven and sprinkle with lemon juice.

9   Using slotted spoon, arrange a portion of scallops on each bed of spinach and top with sauce. Garnish with orange peel, if desired.

White Wine Sauce

60 ml (2 fl oz) dry white wine
1 tablespoon dry sherry
1 tablespoon sherry vinegar
60 ml (2 fl oz) fresh orange juice
2 teaspoons minced shallot
125 g (4 oz) unsalted butter, chilled
Salt and freshly ground pepper

1   In medium-size non-aluminium saucepan, combine wine, sherry, vinegar, orange juice, and shallots. Bring to a boil over medium-high heat and reduce, stirring with wooden spoon, until about 2 tablespoons of syrupy liquid remain, 3 to 4 minutes. Reduce heat to very low.

2   Whisk in chilled butter, 1 tablespoon at a time. Season with salt and pepper to taste.

3   Pour sauce through sieve to remove shallots. Cover and keep warm over very low heat until ready to serve.

Spicy Spinach Sauté

500 g (1 lb) spinach
100 ml (3 fl oz) olive oil
1 level tablespoon minced garlic
1/4 teaspoon Cayenne pepper, or 1/2 teaspoon red pepper flakes
Salt and freshly ground pepper

1   Stem spinach leaves. Rinse thoroughly under cold running water, drain in colander, and dry in salad spinner or pat dry with paper towels.

2   In large sauté pan, heat half the oil over medium-low heat. Add half the spinach leaves and turn heat to medium-high. Add half the garlic and cook, tossing with 2 wooden spoons, until oil begins to crackle, about 1 minute. Add 4 tablespoons water and toss. Add half the Cayenne pepper and salt

and pepper to taste and continue to toss until spinach is wilted, 4 to 5 minutes. Transfer to sieve and press with back of spoon to extract excess liquid. Place in large heatproof bowl and keep warm in SLOW oven. Repeat with remaining ingredients.

3   Divide among individual plates, forming bed for scallops.

Wild Mushroom Salad with Basil and Mint

125 g (4 oz) arugula or watercress leaves
125 g (4 oz) lamb's tongue, or other young lettuce leaves
15 g (1/2 oz) basil leaves
2 level tablespoons mint leaves
300 g (10 oz) fresh wild mushrooms, preferably chanterelles, shiitake, enokitake, or fresh cultivated mushrooms
250 ml (8 fl oz) olive oil
3 shallots, peeled and thinly sliced
Juice of 1 lemon
Salt and freshly ground black pepper
2 tablespoons white wine vinegar

1   Rinse arugula, lamb's tongue, basil, and mint, and dry in salad spinner or pat dry with paper towels. Place in large bowl and set aside.

2   Wipe mushrooms clean with damp paper towels. With chef's knife, slice mushrooms into 1 1/2 cm (3/4 inch) strips.

3   In large sauté pan, heat 125 ml (4 fl oz) oil over medium-high heat. Add mushrooms and sauté, stirring with wooden spatula, just until tender. Stir in lemon juice and season mixture with salt and pepper to taste. Transfer mushroom mixture to bowl.

4   Using 2 wooden spoons, toss the salad greens with the remaining oil and the vinegar. Season with salt and pepper to taste.

5   Divide greens among 4 dinner plates, arranging them on one side of plate, and top each bed of greens with a portion of mushrooms.

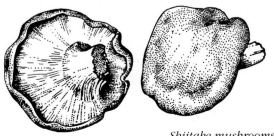

Shiitake mushrooms

49

Mussels and Shrimp in Coconut Cream with Mint
Stuffed Kohlrabi

Thick coconut cream, blended with heavy cream, vermouth, and water, makes a sweet base for this unusual seafood combination. You can buy canned coconut cream in Oriental groceries and many supermarkets. Select snow peas that are very crisp and fresh-looking, and refrigerate them unwashed in a perforated plastic bag until you are ready to cook them. If fresh mint is not available, the cook recommends fresh basil or parsley.

Kohlrabi, a member of the cabbage family, is a green bulb with long leafy stalks and slightly sweet, crunchy flesh. Select unblemished bulbs and refrigerate them in a perforated plastic bag. To

hollow out the kohlrabi after cooking, first cool the bulb under cold running water and then, holding it in the palm of of one hand, carve out the centre with a sharp paring knife.

For the wild mushrooms, choose one from among the following: Golden-coloured chanterelles, shaped like slender curved trumpets, are delicately flavoured. Dark-brown shiitake mushrooms have velvety, thick caps with edges that are curled under when fresh. Enokitake resemble tiny, creamy-white umbrellas.

There is no substitute for kohlrabi for this recipe.

What to drink
A full-bodied white wine is in order; try a Chardonnay or Pinot Blanc from California.

Start-to-Finish Steps
One hour ahead: If preparing homemade coconut cream, combine 60 g (2 oz) packaged shredded coconut with 125 ml (4 fl oz) boiling milk in medium-size bowl. Soak 20 to 30 minutes. Transfer to food processor or blender and process 4 to 5 minutes, or until smooth. Strain through a very fine sieve set over soaking bowl. With your hand, squeeze the pulp left in the sieve until you have extracted as much liquid as possible. Discard pulp and set aside liquid.

Fifteen to 20 minutes ahead: If using a porcini for kohlrabi recipe, place in small bowl and soak in warm water to cover.

1 Follow mussels recipe steps 1 to 4.
2 While mussels are steaming, mince thyme for kohlrabi recipe and chop mint for mussels recipe. Follow mussels recipe step 5.
3 Follow kohlrabi recipe step 1.
4 While water is coming to a boil, follow kohlrabi recipe steps 2 to 5.
5 While kohlrabi are cooking, follow mussels recipe steps 6 to 8.
6 While poaching liquid is reducing, drain kohlrabi and follow recipe step 6.
7 Follow mussels recipe step 9 and kohlrabi recipe steps 7 to 10.
8 Follow mussels recipe steps 10 to 15.
9 Follow kohlrabi recipe step 11, mussels recipe step 16, and serve together.

For an attractive presentation, arrange the mussels and shrimp on a pinwheel of crisp snow peas and garnish each serving with a mussel shell. Serve the stuffed kohlrabi, sprinkled with minced thyme, on the side.

Mussels and Shrimp in Coconut Cream with Mint

1¹/₂ kg (3 lbs) mussels
500 g (1 lb) shrimp
350 ml (12 fl oz) dry vermouth
2 to 3 tablespoons cream of coconut, preferably
    homemade, or canned
250 ml (8 fl oz) heavy cream
2 large or 4 small shallots
1 level tablespoon chopped fresh mint
Freshly ground white pepper
Salt
250 g (¹/₂ lb) snow peas
Fresh mint sprigs (optional)

1   Scrub mussels well and remove beards.
2   Peel and devein shrimp.
3   In stockpot, bring vermouth and 175 ml (6 fl oz) water to a boil. Reduce to a simmer.
4   Add mussels, cover and cook, stirring occasionally, until they open, 4 to 5 minutes.
5   With slotted spoon, transfer mussels to large bowl, discarding any that have not opened.
6   In colander lined with triple thickness of cheesecloth or cloth napkin, strain mussel poaching liquid over deep skillet.
7   Shell mussels, reserving 2 or 3 shells per serving for garnish. Set mussels aside.
8   Over high heat, reduce mussel poaching liquid to about 175 ml (6 fl oz), about 10 minutes. Reduce heat to medium-high.
9   For sauce, add coconut cream and heavy cream to reduced liquid. Stirring with wooden spoon, reduce by one-third, about 10 to 15 minutes.
10 Add shrimp and poach, until they turn pink, about 3 minutes.
11 While shrimp are poaching, peel shallots and slice thinly.
12 Add mussels to sauce. Add shallots, chopped mint, and pepper to taste, and stir to combine. Remove skillet from heat, cover, and keep warm until ready to serve.
13 In saucepan used for kohlrabi, bring 1¹/₄ ltrs (2 pts) salted water to a boil.
14 While water is coming to a boil, rinse snow peas under cold running water. Snap off ends and remove strings.
15 Add snow peas to boiling water, return water to a boil, and immediately pour snow peas under cold running water and drain. Refresh snow peas under cold running water and drain.
16 With slotted spoon, remove shrimp and mussels from sauce. Divide among 4 dinner plates. Top

each portion with sauce and surround with pinwheel' of snow peas. Arrange a few reserved mussel shells, open side down, near mussels and shrimp and garnish with fresh mint sprigs.

Stuffed Kohlrabi

1 red bell pepper
125 g (¹/₄ lb) fresh wild mushrooms, preferably
    chanterelles, shiitake, enokitake, or 60 g (2 oz)
    dried porcini, reconstituted (fresh cultivated may
    be substituted)
Medium-size Spanish onion (about 250 g (¹/₂ llb))
1 large or 2 small shallots
4 small kohlrabi (about 500 g (1 lb) total weight))
4 tablespoons virgin olive oil
1 level tablespoon unsalted butter
Salt
Freshly ground black pepper
¹/₂ teaspoon minced fresh thyme, preferably, or
    parsley

1   In medium-size saucepan, bring 2 ltrs (3 pts) water to a boil.
2   Core, seed, halve, and dice red pepper.
3   If using fresh mushrooms, wipe clean with damp paper towels and mince. If using porcini, drain, discard soaking liquid, pat dry, and mince.
4   Peel and dice onion. Peel and mince shallots.
5   Trim kohlrabi and plunge into boiling water. Boil just until point of sharp knife pierces them easily, about 20 minutes.
6   Preheat oven to SLOW. In large sauté pan, heat 2 tablespoons oil over medium heat. Add red pepper and sauté until soft, 3 to 5 minutes. With slotted spoon, transfer to a small bowl.
7   Add butter to pan. When butter has melted, add onion and sauté over medium heat until soft, about 5 minutes. With slotted spoon, transfer to another small bowl.
8   Add remaining 2 tablespoons oil to pan. Add mushrooms and shallots, and sauté over medium heat 3 to 4 minutes, or until shallots are translucent and mushrooms have softened slightly. With slotted spoon, transfer to third small bowl. Season each mixture with salt and pepper to taste.
9   With paring knife, cut concentric circles in top of each kohlrabi to make shell about 5 mm (¹/₄ inch) thick, taking care not to break sides or puncture bottom.
10 Fill each shell with layers of pepper, onion, and mushroom-shallot mixture. Transfer to heatproof platter and keep warm in oven until ready to serve.
11 With chef's knife, carefully halve kohlrabies lengthwise. Sprinkle with minced thyme and serve.

<table>
<tr><td>

</td><td>

Clams in Sesame-Ginger Sauce
Fettuccine with Garlic and Oil
Mixed Vegetables, Oriental Style

</td></tr>
</table>

This meal features two different Oriental-style recipes. The stir-fried clams, water chestnuts, and daikon are served on a bed of fettuccine and accompanied by a second stir-fry dish of snow peas, bean sprouts, and julienned vegetables.

Daikon, a crisp Japanese white radish, is available year-round in Oriental groceries and some supermarkets. Look for canned lychees in Oriental groceries or speciality food shops. Buy only an Oriental brand of sesame oil; the cold-pressed Middle Eastern variety is not a substitute.

What to drink

A California or Alsatian Gewürztraminer would match the spiciness in this menu; a Riesling would harmonize with the slight sweetness of the sauce.

Start-to-Finish Steps

1 Follow clams recipe step 1.
2 Follow vegetables recipe steps 1 and 2.
3 Follow clams recipe step 2 and fettuccine recipe steps 1 and 2.
4 While pasta water is coming to a boil, follow vegetables recipe step 3 and clams recipe steps 3 to 6.
5 Follow fettuccine recipe steps 3 and 4, and vegetables recipe steps 4 and 5.
6 Follow fettuccine recipe step 5.
7 Follow clams recipe steps 7 to 10, vegetables recipe step 6, and serve.

Clams in Sesame-Ginger Sauce

24 clams
250 g (½ lb) daikon, if available, or white radishes
12 scallions
250 g (8 oz) can water chestnuts
625 g (20 oz) can lychees
1 tablespoon cornstarch
3 tablespoons Chinese sesame oil
1 tablespoon finely grated ginger
1 tablespoon minced garlic
60 ml (2 fl oz) dry sherry
2 tablespoons soy sauce

1 Scrub clams and rinse thoroughly to rid them of sand. In large stockpot or steamer unit, bring 1 cm (½ inch) water to a boil. Add clams and steam, covered, 5 to 7 minutes.
2 With slotted spoon, transfer clams to colander.
3 When clams are cool enough to handle, discard

any that have not opened, and set remaining clams aside. Pour off cooking water from pot, return clams to pot, cover, and keep warm.

4 Peel daikon and cut into thin strips 5 cm (2 in) long.

5 Rinse scallions and pat dry. Trim off root ends and most of green. Slit each scallion in half lengthwise.

6 Drain water chestnuts and lychees, and set aside. In small bowl, blend cornstarch with 1 tablespoon cold water.

7 Heat wok or skillet used for vegetables over medium-high heat for 30 seconds. Add oil. When hot, add daikon, scallions, and water chestnuts, and stir-fry 4 minutes.

8 Add ginger, garlic, sherry, and soy sauce, and toss 1 minute. Add clams and lychees, and stir-fry 1 minute.

9 Add cornstarch mixture to pan a few drops at a time, stirring constantly, until clam mixture reaches desired thickness. You may not need all the cornstarch.

10 Top each portion of fettuccine with a serving of clams in their shells.

Fettuccine with Garlic and Oil

Salt
125 ml (4 fl oz) plus 1 tablespoon virgin olive oil
1 egg
250 to 350 g (1/2 to 3/4 lb) fresh fettuccine, preferably, or dried
1 level tablespoon finely minced garlic
30 g (1 oz) grated Parmesan cheese
1 level tablespoon chopped parsley
Freshly ground pepper

1 Preheat oven to SLOW. In large covered saucepan, over high heat, bring 2½ ltrs (4 pts) water, 1 tablespoon salt, and 1 tablespoon olive oil to a boil.

2 In small bowl, beat egg with fork just until blended.

3 Add fettuccine to boiling water and cook 2 to 3 minutes for fresh, 8 to 12 minutes for dried, or just until *al dente*.

4 While pasta is cooking, warm 4 plates in oven.

5 Drain fettuccine in colander. Return hot pasta to pan. Add remaining olive oil, and toss until evenly coated. Add egg, garlic, Parmesan, parsley, and salt and pepper to taste, and toss until combined. Divide among warmed plates and return to oven until ready to serve.

Mixed Vegetables, Oriental Style

250 g (1/2 lb) snow peas
2 medium-size carrots (about 150 g (5 oz))
Medium-size parsnip (about 125 g (1/4 lb))
Medium-size leek (about 125 g (1/4 lb))
2½ tablespoons olive oil
125 g (1/4 lb) bean sprouts, rinsed and drained
2 teaspoons minced garlic
1½ tablespoons soy sauce
1 level tablespoon grated orange peel
1 level tablespoon unsalted butter

1 In colander, rinse snow peas, drain, and pat dry with paper towels. Pinch off stem ends and pull off strings.

2 Peel carrots and parsnip, and cut into 5 mm (1/4 inch) thick julienne strips.

3 Thoroughly rinse leek. Trim off root end and green part, and discard. With chef's knife, cut white part into 5 mm (1/4 inch) thick julienne strips.

4 Heat wok or large skillet over medium-high heat for 30 seconds. Add oil, tilting pan to coat surface evenly. When oil is hot, add the julienned vegetables and bean sprouts, and toss until well coated. Reduce heat to medium.

5 Add snow peas, garlic, and soy sauce, and stir-fry just until vegetables are crisp-tender, 4 to 5 minutes. Turn into heatproof bowl and keep warm in oven. Wipe out pan.

6 Add orange peel and butter, and toss until blended.

Kathleen Kenny Sanderson

Menu 1
(*Right*)
Seafood Soup Provençale
Chèvre Florentine
Garlic Bread

As Kathleen Kenny Sanderson explains, 'Most people are afraid of cooking with seafood because they do not understand how to handle it.' But, in fact, preparing seafood should be a particular pleasure. In each of the menus here, the cook employs one of the standard French techniques – she poaches the fish and shellfish in Menu 1, sautées the trout in Menu 2, and both poaches and bakes the sea bass in Menu 3 – then improvises to make each recipe her own. Consequently, all her menus have French overtones, even if she uses American products. If you cook all three of these menus, you will have mastered three essential techniques of fish cookery.

The fish stew of Menu 1 resembles the classic bouillabaisse of the Mediterranean city Marseilles. However, this version uses only four kinds of fish and shellfish rather than the traditional variety of twelve or more. The trout of Menu 2, served with saffron rice rather than the more typical French accompaniment, boiled potatoes. For Menu 3, the sea bass, served with a fresh fennel-butter sauce, is accompanied by a garden salad of four distinctive greens.

Seafood soup provençale makes an impressive main-course offering for this informal meal. Serve the spinach salad with goat cheese and a chunk of garlic bread on the same plate. Offer guests extra bread in a napkin-lined basket.

**Seafood Soup Provençale
Chèvre Florentine
Garlic Bread**

Kathleen uses two varieties each of shellfish and fish for her substantial stew.

Pernod, a French liqueur, is often used in bouillabaisse because its delicate anise flavour enhances seafood.

Chèvre Florentine, a goat's cheese and spinach salad, is unusual and simple to prepare.

What to drink
Choose an Italian Verdicchio or a French Muscadet.

Start-to-Finish Steps
1 For bread recipe, remove butter from refrigerator.
2 Follow chèvre recipe steps 1 to 3.
3 Follow soup recipe steps 1 to 5. While vegetables cook, follow bread recipe steps 1 and 2.
4 Follow soup recipe step 6. While soup is cooking, follow garlic bread recipe steps 3 and 4.
5 Follow soup recipe step 8 and chèvre recipe steps 4 to 6.
6 Follow soup recipe step 8 and chèvre recipe step 7.
7 Follow soup recipe step 9.
8 Follow chèvre recipe step 8 and bread recipe step 5.
9 Follow chèvre recipe step 9, soup recipe step 10, and serve with garlic bread.

Seafood Soup Provençale

3 large carrots
Large yellow onion
2 stalks celery
12 medium-size shrimp
12 clams or mussels
250 g (1/2 lb) fillet of monkfish
250 g (1/2 lb) fillet of cod, halibut, or sea bass, cut
    2 1/2 cm (1 inch) thick
60 ml (2 fl oz) virgin olive oil
175 ml (6 fl oz) dry white wine
2 tablespoons Pernod
500 g (16 oz) can Italian plum tomatoes
1 bay leaf
Salt and freshly ground pepper

1 Cut carrots, celery, and onion into 5 mm (1/4 inch) slices. Cut onion rings crosswise into semi-circles.
2 Shell and devein shrimp.
3 Scrub clams or mussels. Debeard mussels. Rinse thoroughly and discard any that have open shells.
4 Wipe and cut fish into 4 cm (1 1/2 inch) squares.
5 Heat oil over medium-high heat. Reduce heat to medium. Sauté vegetables, for 2 to 3 minutes.

6 Add wine and Pernod, and cook 2 to 3 minutes.
7 Add tomatoes, bay leaf, and season. Bring to a boil, then simmer, uncovered, 4 to 5 minutes.
8 Add shrimp and clams, and simmer 3 minutes.
9 Add fish and simmer just until firm, about 5 minutes.
10 Remove bay leaf and serve in 4 individual bowls.

Chèvre Florentine

2 cloves garlic
125 ml (4 fl oz) virgin olive oil
1/2 teaspoon crushed red pepper
250 g (1/2 lb) chèvre, or feta cheese
500 g (1 lb) spinach
Medium-size red bell pepper
2 shallots
3 tablespoons white wine vinegar

1 Peel garlic and mince finely.
2 Combine oil, garlic, and crushed pepper, and sauté until garlic turns golden brown, about 2 minutes.
3 Slice chèvre evenly into 8 rounds and place on plate. Transfer 5 tbsps oil into bowl and spoon remaining oil, with garlic and red pepper, over chèvre. Set aside.
4 Wash and dry spinach, discard stems.
5 Wash and dry red bell pepper. Core, halve, and seed pepper. Cut into 1 cm (1/2 inch) dice and set aside.
6 Peel and mince shallots.
7 In bowl, combine spinach, red pepper, and shallots.
8 Toss salad with reserved oil and then with vinegar.
9 Divide salad among 4 plates, arranging on 1/3 of each plate, and top each with 2 slices marinated chèvre.

Garlic Bread

2 cloves garlic
125 g (4 oz) unsalted butter, at room temperature
1 level tbsp minced fresh basil, or 1 tsp dried
1 level tbsp minced fresh oregano, or 1 tsp dried
1/2 tsp freshly ground pepper
1 loaf French or Italian bread, white or whole wheat

1 Preheat grill
2 Peel garlic and mince finely.
3 In small bowl, mash together butter, garlic, basil, oregano, and pepper until thoroughly combined.
4 Halve bread lengthwise and spread cut sides with butter mixture. Place on tray, buttered sides up.
5 Grill bread until it is lightly toasted, 1 to 2 mins.

Rainbow Trout
Julienned Vegetables
Saffron Rice Mould

Fresh rainbow trout is a delicacy and is at its best when just caught. Store fresh trout packed in ice in the refrigerator until you are ready to cook it. Frozen trout is commonly available but may have lost some of its delicate flavour. Defrost frozen trout overnight in the refrigerator.

What to drink

A good-quality white Burgundy, such as a Meursault, or a fine California Chardonnay is right for this trout classic.

Start-to-Finish Steps

1   Follow rice recipe steps 1 to 5.
2   While rice is cooking, wash, dry, and chop parsley for trout and rice recipes, and follow trout recipe steps 1 to 5.
3   While first batch of trout is cooking, follow vegetables recipe step 1 and rice recipe step 6.
4   Follow trout recipe step 6.
5   Follow rice recipe step 7 and, after turning trout, vegetables recipe steps 2 and 3.
6   Follow trout recipe steps 7 to 9, rice recipe step 8, and serve with vegetables.

Garnish the fish with parsley sprigs and halved lemon 'wheels.' Colourful saffron rice and julienned vegetables accompany the fish.

Rainbow Trout

2 lemons
4 whole rainbow trout, or perch (each about 250-300 g (8-10 oz each), or eight 7½-10 cm (3 to 4 oz each) thick fillets 100 g-125 g (3-4 oz each)
45-60 g (1½-2 oz) flour
Salt and freshly ground pepper
60 ml (2 fl oz) vegetable oil
100 ml (3 fl oz) dry white wine
15 g (½ oz) chopped parsley, plus additional sprigs for garnish
125 g (4 oz) unsalted butter

1 Preheat oven to 200°C (400°F or Mark 6).
2 Squeeze enough lemon juice to measure 100 ml (3 fl oz) juice and slice lemon 'wheels' for garnish.
3 If using whole fish, remove fins and, with knife, gently scrape skin to remove scales. Wipe whole fish or fillets with damp paper towels and pat dry.
4 On large plate, mix flour with salt and pepper to taste. Roll fish or dip fillets in flour to coat lightly.
5 In large skillet, heat 2 tablespoons oil over medium-high heat. Add 2 whole fish or 4 fillets. Cook whole fish 4 minutes per side, fillets 2 to 3 minutes per side, turning with spatula. Transfer to plates and place in oven.
6 Repeat cooking process with remaining fish.
7 Pour off excess oil. Add lemon juice, wine, and parsley to skillet. Over medium-high heat, reduce liquid by about half, about 3 minutes.
8 Add butter, 1 tablespoon at a time, whisking constantly.

9 Remove plates from oven, pour sauce over fish, and garnish with parsley sprigs and halved lemon 'wheels'.

Julienned Vegetables

250 g (½ lb) carrots, peeled
250 g (½ lb) yellow squash
250 g (½ lb) courgettes
Large red bell pepper, cored and seeded (optional)
2 level tablespoons unsalted butter
60 ml (2 fl oz) chicken stock
1 level tablespoon chopped fresh dill, or 1 teaspoon dried
Salt and freshly ground pepper

1 With chef's knife julienne all vegetables, cutting into 7½ cm (3 inch) matchsticks.
2 In large skillet, melt butter over medium heat. Add vegetables and toss with wooden spatula until completely coated with butter. Add chicken stock and dill, and cook over medium high heat, stirring, until just crisp tender, 2 to 3 minutes. Season with salt and pepper to taste.
3 Keep warm over very low heat.

Saffron Rice Mould

1 bunch scallions
500 ml (1 pt) chicken stock
½ to 1 teaspoon loosely packed saffron threads
Large red bell pepper, cored and seeded (optional)
1 tablespoon vegetable oil
175 g (6 oz) long-grain rice
Salt and freshly ground pepper
1 level tablespoon chopped parsley (optional)

1 Wash scallions and pat dry with paper towels. Trim scallions and dice enough to measure 60 g (2 oz).
2 In small saucepan, bring chicken stock to a boil over medium-high heat.
3 With mortar and pestle, pulverize saffron threads.
4 In medium-size sauté pan, heat oil over medium-high heat. Add scallions and sauté 1 minute. Add rice and saffron, and sauté, stirring, 1 minute.
5 Add boiling stock to rice mixture and add salt and pepper to taste. Return to a boil over medium-high heat, then reduce to a simmer. Cover and cook 18 minutes.
6 Turn off heat. Let sit 10 minutes.
7 Lightly butter four 500 g (1 lb) ramekins or custard cups.
8 Pack rice into ramekins, and then invert and unmould onto plates. Garnish with parsley, if desired.

Sea Bass with Fennel-Butter Sauce
Warm Potato Salad
Garden Salad with Mustard Vinaigrette

You can serve sea bass with the skin on, but the cook suggests that you skin it before eating, although the skin is edible. The butter sauce contains chopped fresh fennel, also known as *finiccio*. Fennel has a bulbous base and feathery green leaves. Select bulbs that are firm and have no soft or brownish spots. If fresh fennel is unavailable, substitute fennel or anise seeds and crush them to release their flavour.

A warm potato salad and a chilled garden salad accompany the sea bass. For the warm salad, select evenly sized new red potatoes. Be sure they are firm and have smooth unblemished skins. Pour the dressing on while potatoes are still warm so that it soaks in.

The garden salad combines four leafy vegetables, watercress, radicchio, arugula, and endive, with contrasting colours and textures. All salad greens should be wrapped in plastic bags and refrigerated.

What to drink

A firm, acidic wine is what this menu calls for, and there are several candidates: a California Sauvignon Blanc, a small-château Graves from Bordeaux, a Pouilly Fumé from the Loire, or an Italian Greco di Tufo.

Start-to-Finish Steps

1 Follow potato salad recipe steps 1 to 3.
2 While potatoes are boiling, follow fennel-butter sauce recipe steps 1 and 2.
3 While wine is reducing, follow garden salad recipe steps 1 to 4 and sea bass recipe step 1.
4 Follow fennel-butter sauce recipe step 3 and potato salad recipe step 4.
5 Follow sea bass recipe steps 2 to 5.
6 While fish is baking, follow garden salad recipe steps 5 to 7 and potato salad recipe step 5.
7 Follow fennel-butter sauce recipe step 4, sea bass recipe steps 6 and 7, garden salad recipe step 8, potato salad recipe step 6, and serve.

Sea Bass with Fennel-Butter Sauce

4 fillets of sea bass, sea trout, or halibut (each about 250 g (8 oz)), with or without skin
1 level tablespoon unsalted butter, approximately
125 ml (4 fl oz) dry white wine
Salt
Freshly ground pepper

Silvery sea bass topped with fennel-butter sauce and garnished with a sprig of watercress makes an elegant company dish. Serve the potato salad with the fish, and the garden salad separately.

Fennel-butter sauce (see following recipe)
Watercress sprigs for garnish (optional)

1 Preheat oven to 200°C (400°F or Mark 6).
2 Wipe fish with damp paper towels.
3 Butter flameproof 18 cm by 30 cm (7 by 12 inch) baking dish.
4 In baking dish, bring 500 ml (1 pt) water and wine to a boil over medium-high heat. Add fish and salt and pepper to taste, and cover tightly with aluminium foil.
5 Bake until fish flakes easily when tested with fork, 5 to 6 minutes.
6 While fish is baking, warm dinner plates under hot running water and dry.
7 With metal spatula, transfer fillets to warm dinner plates. Top with fennel-butter sauce and garnish with watercress sprigs, if desired. Skin fillets before eating, if desired.

Fennel Butter Sauce

Medium-size fennel bulb, or 1 level tablespoon
   fennel seeds or anise seeds
1/2 bunch scallions
350 ml (12 fl oz) dry white wine
250 g (8 oz) unsalted butter

1 Rinse fennel, trim off ends and feathery greens, and dice enough of bulb to measure 125 g (4 oz). Rinse and trim scallions and finely chop enough to measure 60 g (2 oz).
2 In medium-size saucepan, combine fennel, scallions, and wine, and bring to a boil over high heat. Lower heat to medium-high and reduce liquid until wine is almost evaporated, 8 to 10 minutes, taking care that vegetables do not singe.
3 Reduce heat to very low, and whisk in butter, 1 tablespoon at a time, until completely incorporated. Cover pan partially and turn off heat, but leave pan on burner until ready to serve.
4 Whisk sauce to recombine.

Warm Potato Salad

750 g (1 1/2 lb) new red potatoes
1 lemon
15 g (1/2 oz) chopped parsley
30 g (1 oz) finely chopped chives or scallion greens
100 ml (3 fl oz) vegetable oil
Salt
Freshly ground pepper

1 Wash potatoes, but do not peel.

2 In medium-size saucepan fitted with steamer, bring 5 cm (2 inches) water to a boil. Place potatoes in steamer, cover, and steam just until potatoes can be easily penetrated with tip of sharp knife, 15 to 20 minutes, depending on size of potatoes.
3 Squeeze enough lemon to measure 2 tablespoons juice. Wash parsley and chives or scallions and pat dry. Chop enough parsley to measure 15 g (1/2 oz). Trim chives or scallion greens, and finely chop enough to measure 30 g (1 oz).
4 Drain potatoes in colander and return to pan off heat.
5 In small bowl, combine parsley, chives, and lemon juice. Add oil, salt and pepper to taste, and whisk until blended. Set aside.
6 Slice potatoes and arrange on dinner plates alongside fish. Spoon dressing over warm potatoes.

Garden Salad with Mustard Vinaigrette

1 head radicchio or small head escarole
Medium-size bunch watercress
Small bunch arugula
1 head endive
1 egg
250 ml (8 fl oz) vegetable oil
1 tablespoon whole-grain mustard
Dash of Worcestershire sauce
Salt
Freshly ground pepper

1 Place salad bowls in freezer to chill
2 Separate radicchio leaves and discard core. Remove stems from watercress. Trim arugula stems. Wash radicchio, watercress, and arugula, and dry in salad spinner or pat dry with paper towels.
3 Remove bruised outer leaves of endive. Slice 1 cm (1/2 inch) off base of endive, then slice endive in half crosswise and lengthwise, and separate leaves.
4 Remove salad bowls from freezer and divide greens among them. Cover and refrigerate until ready to serve.
5 Separate egg, placing yolk in small bowl and reserving white for another use. Whisk yolk until thick and lemon-coloured, 1 to 2 minutes. Beating constantly, add oil in thin stream until completely incorporated.
6 In another small bowl, combine mustard, vinegar, and Worcestershire sauce, and stir until blended.
7 Slowly drizzle mustard mixture into egg mixture, whisking constantly. Season with salt and pepper to taste. Set aside.
8 Toss salad with mustard vinaigrette and serve.

Meet the Cooks

Leslie Land

Food writer and consultant Leslie Land, lives on the Maine coast. She began her cookery career during college when she worked as a part time caterer. She now writes a weekly food column and contributes articles to *Food & Wine* and *Cuisine*.

Paul Neuman and Stacy Bogdonoff

Stacy Bogdonoff graduated from the Culinary Institute of America, then attended advanced classes at L'Ecole de Cuisine La Varenne in Paris. Paul Neuman apprenticed with a private caterer. Together they own, operate and cook for Neuman&Bogdonoff, a food store and catering service in New York City.

Patricia Unterman

As co-owner of a restaurant in San Francisco, which specializes in fresh sea food, Patricia Unterman creates new fish recipes daily, experimenting with uncommon varieties. Patricia Unterman is also the restaurant critic for the *San Francisco Chronicle*.

Josephine Araldo

Josephine Araldo was born in Brittany. She attended Le Cordon Bleu for four and a half years and cooked professionally in Paris. After moving to Northern California, she worked first as a private chef and then conducted cookery courses.

Bruce Cliborne

Chef, food stylist, recipe developer, and caterer Bruce Cliborne experiments with elements of every kind of cuisine. Bruce Cliborne was a contributing author of and food stylist for the *Soho Charcuterie Cookbook*.

Kathleen Kenny Sanderson

Kathlenn Kenny Sanderson, who lives in New York, is a graduate of the California Culinary Academy in San Francisco. She cooked at L'Escargot in San Francisco, and later was personal chef for the Robert Kennedy family. Besides teaching cookery, she is the Food Editor and Test Kitchen Director at *Restaurant Business* magazine.

A Wealth of Herbs

Increasingly, herbs are arriving in the markets fresh; the proliferation of health stores and other specialist shops has widened choice, and many cooks with gardens have taken to raising their own. Recent ethnic influences have called attention to once seemingly esoteric herbs. Coriander, for one, is at last gaining deserved popularity in Europe, although cooks in Asia and the Middle East have been using it for centuries.

Anyone wishing to dry fresh herbs can tie them loosely in a bundle and hang them upside down in a cool, dark, well-ventilated place for several weeks. When the leaves are completely dried, strip them from the stems and store them in an airtight container.

Two swifter methods of preserving herbs make use of the microwave oven and the freezer. To microwave herbs, place five or six sprigs at a time between paper towels and microwave them on high for 1 to 3 minutes until the leaves are brittle. Store the leaves loosely in airtight jars.

To freeze herbs, rinse the sprigs and pat them dry. Strip the leaves off the stems and put them into a heavy-duty plastic bag. Gently flatten the bag to force out the air, seal the bag tightly, and place it in your freezer. Use the leaves as the need arises.

Basil (also called sweet basil): This fragrant herb, with its underlying flavour of anise and hint of clove, goes particularly well with tomato.

Chervil: The small, lacy leaves of this herb have a taste akin to parsley with a touch of anise. It is good in salads and salad dressings. Chervil is popular in France, where it is often an ingredient in herb mixtures, including *fines herbes*. When used in cooking, chervil should be added at the end, lest its subtle flavour be lost.

Chives: The smallest of the onions, chives grow in grassy clumps. When finely cut, the hollow leaves contribute their delicate, oniony flavour to fresh salads and raw vegetables. Chives should always be used fresh, as dried ones are virtually tasteless.

Coriander (also called cilantro): The serrated leaves of the coriander plant impart a distinctive fragrance and a flavour that is both mildly sweet and bitter. Coriander leaves should be used fresh or added at the end of cooking if their flavour is to be appreciated fully.

Dill: A sprightly herb with feathery leaves, dill enhances cucumber and many other fresh vegetables, as well as fish and shellfish. When used in cooking, dill should be added towards the end of the process to preserve its delicate flavour. Both dill seeds and dill leaves can be